MINISTRY IN THE MILK BARN:

A FARMER'S TALK WITH THE LORD

by

Tom Harrington

Tom Harrington

27 Alli Paige Drive Vilonia AR

501-472-5295

painehall@yahoo.com

Ministryinthe milkbarn.wordpress.com

Foreword

Thank you for your interest in *Ministry in the Milk Barn: A Farmer's Talk with The Lord.* This book has been something that I almost fought. I doubted the quality, my ability, and people's interest, but then God kicked me in the head, and I knew that I couldn't hide His word and the talents that He has given me.

You will find that I use lots of personal experiences. I've been a farmer and have a heart for watching things grow and prosper. I used my love of growing things to teach agriculture; but my goal was to teach God's love and greatness as I tried to make my students the best they could be. I've also been a cowboy and a rodeo announcer. I've seen a lot of country, and you'll find stories about all my experiences in these devotionals. You'll also see the love and pride that I have for the United States of America. I talk about family, friends, life, and death. This is a glimpse into my life that God has inspired me to write about. I hope that, through these devotionals, you will find blessings from the Lord and strengthen your relationship with Him. The devotionals aren't grouped in any particular order, but just in the way I felt that God wants them. Enjoy!

The first seven devotionals are words from The Lord that I've already talked about and shared with my small community group in 2017. Unless I indicate otherwise, all Bible verses are from the New Living Translation (NLT)[1] *Holy Bible.* God speaks to each of us in a still small voice. It's amazing how just one word can drive us.

Rest

"Rest when you're weary.
Refresh and renew yourself, your body, your
mind, your spirit. Then get back to work."
– Ralph Marston

In our daily lives we are on the go most all day and not just one or two days, but *every* day. There is always work to do, meetings to attend, and many other kinds of things to do. We get tired. I remember when I was farming that there was always something to do. One thing I learned very early was that I had to have time to rest, because if I didn't, eventually I wouldn't be able to work at all. "Time to rest" doesn't just mean "time to sleep" it means "time to stop the work and activities and take time to recharge and reflect."

Genesis 2:2. "On the seventh day God had finished his work of creation, so he rested from all his work."

Even God rested. He's all-powerful, all-knowing, and He rested. I don't know if He took a nap or slept much, but I know that He looked over all that He had done. This is reflection time to see what you still need to tackle, what can wait, and what to do next. If we don't reflect, sometimes we can become overwhelmed and frustrated. This is what the enemy is waiting for. Satan will use this chance to cause you to doubt God. He'll make you angry and try to drive a wedge between you and God. It's important to rest, so we can recharge and listen to God.

Hold On

*"Age wrinkles the body.
Quitting wrinkles the soul."*
– Douglas Macarthur

I'm starting to see wrinkles, lines, and gray hair. Some might see them as signs of getting old. I see them as signs of character from a life well-lived. This year, God gave me a word for my life: PERSEVERE. Most anyone who knows me knows that I have persevered my entire life. Quitting doesn't have a big place in my vocabulary or in my mentality – I don't give up much. My wife calls it stubborn. However, there have been times in the recent past that I thought about quitting and giving up on a dream that I've had. *PERSEVERE* came to me at a good time; it was perfectly timed, because it came from God.

Revelation 3:10-11. "Because you have obeyed my command to persevere, I will protect you from the great time of testing that will come upon the whole world to test those who belong to this world. I am coming soon. Hold on to what you have, so that no one will take away your crown."

This is from the message to the church at Philadelphia, but I feel like it speaks to all of our lives.

God never said that life was going to be easy and without hardship. God does say, however, that He will always be with us through those times. The Bible says that we should rejoice when we face troubles in our walk with God. When Satan sees us as strong Christians, he gets mad. He wants to do whatever it takes to belittle God and to break apart our relationship. That's why when things get tough, Satan encourages us to quit and give up. Don't do it! God works in perfect time. Just when it looks like a lost cause, God steps up.

Mercy Walked In[2]
I stood in the court room the judge turn my way
It looks like you're guilty now what do you say
I spoke up your honor I have no defense
But that's when mercy walked in

Mercy walked in and pleaded my case
Called to the stand God's saving grace
The blood was presented that covered my sin
Forgiven when mercy walked in

Praise the Lord

I stood there and wondered how could this be
That someone so guilty had just been set free
My chains were broken I felt born again
The moment that mercy walked in

---

[2] Song by Gordon Mote and Sheri Easter; Songwriters: Stuart Keene Hine. This song appears on the album *Don''t Let Me Miss The Glory (2007)*. Mercy Walked In lyrics © Capitol Christian Music Group.

Ooh

Ministry in the Milk Barn: A Farmer's Talk with The Lord

The blood was presented that covered my sin
Forgiven when mercy walked in.

God is going to be there. He is perfect and so are His plans. He has great blessings for us here on Earth, and the greatest eternal home for us when we persevere.

Adventure

*"All adventures, especially into new territory,
are scary." – Sally Ride*

As the first female astronaut from the USA to be on the space station, I'm sure Sally Ride faced a lot of fear in her adventures. To be honest with you, I can't wrap my mind around going to space and making history like she did. What great experience she had when it was over. Oh the stories that she had. That gets me to thinking about my life and my adventures. I've had some good ones myself, but I know of a man who had some great adventures that were truly life changing for him as well as changed the world for generations to come.

Galatians 1:11-24. "Dear brothers and sisters, I want you to understand that the gospel message I preach is not based on mere human reasoning. I received my message from no human source, and no one taught me. Instead, I received it by direct revelation from Jesus Christ. You know what I was like when I followed the Jewish religion—how I violently persecuted God's church. I did my best to destroy it. I was far ahead of my fellow Jews in my zeal for the traditions of my ancestors. But even before I was born, God chose me and called me by his marvelous grace. Then it pleased him to reveal his Son to me so that I would proclaim the Good News about Jesus to the Gentiles. When this happened, I did not rush out to consult with any human being. Nor did I go up to Jerusalem to consult with those who were apostles before I was. Instead, I went away into Arabia, and later I returned to the city of Damascus. Then three years later, I went to Jerusalem to get to know Peter, and I stayed with him for fifteen days. The only other apostle I met at that time was James, the Lord's brother. I declare before God that what I am writing to you is not a lie. After that visit I went north into the provinces of Syria and Cilicia. And still the churches in Christ that are in Judea didn't know me personally. All they knew was that people were saying, 'The one who used to persecute us is now preaching the very faith he tried to destroy!' And they praised God because of me."

This is a story of Paul. This guy had some awesome adventures. From being blinded by God to all of the churches that he planted, he was a busy guy. When we read through the Bible, Paul was on a couple of ships that wrecked. He was bitten by a snake; and one night, he and Silas were in a jail cell; the Lord wanted them out so He sent an earthquake so strong that the entire jail just about fell down. What stories he could tell!

Does God have adventures like Paul's in store for us? I would think so, but if we don't submit and follow Him, how will we ever know? God has only the best in mind for those who believe in Him, so how can it be a bad thing? I encourage you to seek Him, and the adventures will be out of this world.

Guidance

"We need only obey. There is guidance
for each of us, and by lowly listening
we shall hear the right word."
– Ralph Waldo Emerson

"The older I get, the smarter my dad becomes." We've heard this before, and we've probably all been there. What causes this? The problem is that life is totally opposite from school in the way that we become educated. In school, we have a teacher who gives us guidance through the lessons, and then we take a test. When this happens, we are more able to see and understand the need for guidance and direction, but in life oftentimes, the test comes first and then the lesson. This makes it hard for us to accept guidance, because we don't even know that we are going somewhere.

Proverbs 24:5-6. "The wise are mightier than the strong, and those with knowledge grow stronger and stronger. So don't go to war without wise guidance; victory depends on having many advisers."

One of my favorite movies is *War Room*. I know that it was a little cheesy, but it does demonstrate that we are all at war. We aren't in a war like the military, but we all have our own personal battles. The enemy attacks us trying to make us move away from God. Look what Jesus says here . . .

John 10:10. "The thief's purpose is to steal and kill and destroy. My purpose is to give them a rich and satisfying life."

"To steal, kill, and destroy," that's what we face every single day. The enemy wants to steal our happiness. He wants to kill the faith that we have in Jesus, and he wants to destroy our relationship and spending eternity with God. We are at war!

So what do we do? Where do we turn for guidance in winning this war? We need to find mentors on Earth. This goes back to the part where I said, "the older I get, the smarter my dad becomes." We have to recognize that we can't do life alone, and we need to seek out a wise person. Then we need to look at the last part of the verse from John. Jesus says that His purpose is to give us a rich, satisfying life. Again we have to remember that we aren't meant to do life alone, so when the enemy attacks and we are using the lessons learned, we must also pray without ceasing because when God is with us, who can be against us? Seek His guidance in all that you do. When you do this, His light shines through you so that you may offer guidance to others.

Laughter

"Against the assault of laughter
nothing can stand." – Mark Twain

Today it seems that we have less and less to laugh about. In fact, I have worked with some young people whom I had to tell that it's okay to laugh. I'm not sure why, but it seemed that they were afraid of laughter. If it weren't for laughter, just think how dull our lives would be.

Psalm 126:2-3. "We were filled with laughter, and we sang for joy. And the other nations said, 'What amazing things the Lord has done for them.' Yes, the Lord has done amazing things for us! What joy!"

I make it a point to make people laugh. Especially when I can tell that they are angry and upset. I've heard it said that laughter is the best medicine, but I will add on to that. Laughter will drive the enemy away. What the enemy wants is for us to feel depressed, worried, sad, and angry. If the enemy can get us to this point, he has robbed us of our joy. He wants us to be this way to try and harden our hearts toward God. In the scriptures above, David says that they were filled with laughter and sang with joy. Look what else it says: other nations take notice.

Wow, we show others the greatness of God through our actions and attitude. I think it's important that we seek laughter, because it reminds us of the joy and love that the Lord has shown us. When others in our dark world see us laughing, they see us as a ray of light in God's imagination. Our laughter is an outward expression of the joy and happiness that God gives. Don't be afraid to let your joy and light shine.

Favor

*"Seek not the favor of the multitude; it is
seldom got by honest and lawful means. But
seek the testimony of few; and number not
voices, but weigh them." — Immanuel Kant*

fa·vor

ˈfāvər/

—*noun*

1. approval, support, or liking for someone or
    something "The legislation is viewed with
    favor."

2. an act of kindness beyond what is due or usual
    "I've come to ask you a favor."

—*verb*

1. feel or show approval or preference for
    "slashing public spending is a policy that few
    politicians favor"

2. (often used in polite requests) give someone
    (something that they want) "Please favor me
    with an answer."

What is favor? I think of it as being
someone's go-to person or trusted one. We can think
of it like when we go hunting; most of the time we
don't just grab up any gun and go, but we take the

one that we have faith in, the one that we trust. In rodeo, sometimes we might ride many horses during the year because basically we should be able to do the same thing on every horse. But when the big show is in town, we get on the one horse we trust, love, and get along with the best. We show favor to this horse; it may not be the biggest, fastest, strongest, or be the best looking, but it's the one that is the most reliable, honest, and true to us. When we find favor with God, that's what we are, the ones who are faithful, honest, and true.

Genesis 6:8. "But Noah found favor with the Lord."

It's easy to mix up favor and blessings. Let's look at it this way: favor is who we are, and blessings are what we get. In this verse about Noah, it says that he found favor with the Lord. And if you know the story of Noah, you know that the blessing that he received was that he and his family were spared when all other living things on Earth were destroyed. That's a great blessing, but why did he get these blessings and favor? Because he was faithful to God. Was he perfect? No. Later after the flood, Noah got drunk and laid around naked. We don't have to be perfect. Jesus knows that we can never be that way. However, we can try to be like Jesus in our lives and how we interact with others, along with the faith that we show in the Lord. When we reach the point that the Lord finds favor in us, the blessings will flow.

However, the thing about favor is that God doesn't give it for personal gain, but it's given so that the greatness of God will be shown to others through them. So remember this . . .

Luke 12:48. "But someone who does not know, and then does something wrong, will be punished only lightly. When someone has been given much, much will be required in return; and when someone has been entrusted with much, even more will be required."

When God gives us favor and blessings, we must use them to better His kingdom. However, I think that when you truly find favor in God, like Noah did, we love God and His kingdom more than we love ourselves so it would be only normal for us to grow His kingdom.

To find favor, we must be faithful and true in our relationship with God; the blessings we receive will not only enhance our lives, but will show others the love and awesomeness of God through us. Let your light shine bright when the Lord finds favor in you.

Gather

"Awards become corroded,
friends gather no dust." – Jesse Owens

"Gather" is an exciting word. It means to bring together. The thing about gathering is that oftentimes we have to go hunt for what we are gathering. A rancher who gathers cattle goes out on the range and gets them, and a farmer who gathers crops is out in the fields. This sometimes takes us out of our comfort zone. When we set out to gather things, we can and will experience new things from God.

Matthew 18:19-20. "I also tell you this: If two of you agree here on earth concerning anything you ask, my Father in heaven will do it for you. For where two or three gather together as my followers, I am there among them."

The thing that I first think of when I say the word gather is being out and about, being active. We have often heard that the best sermons are lived and not preached. Just think of all the great things that God can show us when we get out and about. Think what might happen if we get out of our comfort zones and start gathering other believers together. It might be for a fishing trip or just a random act of kindness. As the scripture says, where two or more believers should gather, God will be there. Can you imagine how bright the light can shine from this gathering?

In our world today, there are lots of dark spots. God calls on us to help gather His flock. So don't be afraid to get out of your comfort zone and let Him shine through you. If we do that, it might be like moths to a flame, and believers will come to God's light that you shine.

God has great and different plans for each of us. To live in His favor is exciting. I hope that you can find the courage to keep up the journey.

Ten Seconds in the Saddle or a Lifetime of Just Watching

TEN SECONDS IN THE SADDLE[3]
by Chris LeDoux

Well I'll gladly take ten seconds in the saddle
For a lifetime of watching from the stands.

His Stetson was faded and battered and worn
The stubble of his beard showed flex of gray
His limp was severe cause a leg had been torn
by a bronc in his rodeo days
He hung round the chutes while we waited to
mount
With a vague look of longing in his eyes
He spoke very few words but he made 'em
count
He was broken forgotten but wise
He said life's is just like ridin' broncs it's a battle
Then he rolled a cigarette with shaky hands
Son I'll gladly take ten seconds in the saddle
For a lifetime of watching from the stands

I noticed the cigarette burns on his vest
And the Rembrandt of a dream left in his eyes
The boys said he could have well been the best
Had not fate cheated him of his prize
Oh but I learned a lesson that I never known
From this guy who'd been busted so bad
It's better to ride even if you get throwed

---

[3] Song by Chris LeDoux. This song appears on the album *Western Tunesmith (1979)*. Ten Seconds in the Saddle lyrics © 2018 Genius Media Group Inc.

Than to wind up just wishing you had
He said life's is just like...
Yes I'll gladly take ten seconds in the saddle
For a lifetime of watching from the stands

That has to be one of my favorite songs. Not only does it talk about rodeo, but it tells a good life lesson. While it is a lot safer sitting in the stands than in the arena, what can you gain? Sometimes in life we have to let go of what seems safe to get to a place where we truly experience all of the greatness in life that God has for us. As cowboys we have faith in our ability to be or to do what seems like the impossible, in life we have something much better than cowboy skills, we have Jesus.

Matthew 14:23-31. "After sending them home, he went up into the hills by himself to pray. Night fell while he was there alone. Meanwhile, the disciples were in trouble far away from land, for a strong wind had risen, and they were fighting heavy waves. About three o'clock in the morning Jesus came toward them, walking on the water. When the disciples saw him walking on the water, they were terrified. In their fear, they cried out, 'It's a ghost!' But Jesus spoke to them at once. 'Don't be afraid,' he said. 'Take courage. I am here!' Then Peter called to him, 'Lord, if it's really you, tell me to come to you, walking on the water.' 'Yes, come,' Jesus said. So Peter went over the side of the boat and walked on the water toward Jesus. But when he saw the strong wind and the waves, he was terrified and began to sink. 'Save me, Lord!' he shouted. Jesus immediately reached out and grabbed him. 'You have so little faith,' Jesus said. 'Why did you doubt me?'"

I'll be the first to admit that my faith has faltered at times. If I had just been a little more willing to take a chance, to lean completely on God I'm not sure where I would be. That's something to learn from. As we see above, Peter had doubts. Why this guy had doubt, is beyond me because right before this, Peter watched Jesus take some bread and a couple of fish and feed thousands. When he questioned Jesus and Jesus said come on, you'd think Peter would just walk around like a stroll in the park, but nope! At the first sign of a little trouble, he lets his doubt start to sink him. He was wishing to be sitting on the sidelines watching instead of walking on water.

What could you do if you went for 10 seconds in the saddle? Is there a chance of hitting the dirt? Sure there is! But if you learn from it, you are better for it. That's more than you'll get from watching. In our relationship with God, can we believe that Jesus died for us and still play it safe? I guess you can, but why? Jesus is in control!! What we can learn and experience in only 10 seconds is worth more than two lifetimes of sitting in the stands.

WOW

"Wonder is involuntary praise."
– Edward Young

A week or so ago, I was asked to judge the dairy goats at a fair here in Arkansas. One of the exhibitors commented that I said, "Wow" a lot when each class came into the show ring. I explained to her that I love to see God's greatness, and I was seeing it in these animals and the exhibitors with the love and passion that they showed. I'll just tell you that I love anything in nature or anything agricultural, especially when you see that people have put years of dedicated love and hard work into it. Whether it's a cow, a goat, a horse, a mountain, an ocean, or a small flower, I'm amazed at the great things God creates.

Habakkuk 3:1-2. "This prayer was sung by the prophet Habakkuk: 'I have heard all about you, Lord. I am filled with awe by your amazing works. In this time of our deep need, help us again as you did in years gone by. And in your anger, remember your mercy.'"

One thing that watching things grow does is that it reminds me that God is still very alive and still doing amazing things, not just in cows and in nature, but He is still working and growing each one of us. I recently wrote about removing the weeds from our lives, and now I want you to start thinking about feeding what God is growing in us. Just like our physical bodies, our spiritual selves needs to be fed. How do we do that? Can I get it at Golden Corral? No, but it is easy to get. As you read that Habakkuk sang to God, he worshipped, and prayed. That's one way to get fed. You can study the Bible, go to church, and visit with other believers. Those are all ways to "get fed."

God wants to use each of us to be a part of His great and amazing works, but we can't be amazing if we starve to death. Please, my friends, make time to feed on His gifts so that you can experience His amazing greatness.

Out with the Old

*"Many people look forward to the New Year
for a new start on old habits." – Unknown*

I, for one, was proud to see 2016 go. This year has been one of extreme change, loss, and questions. I had gotten to the point where I didn't like seeing certain people because that meant someone close to me had passed away. I lost an Uncle, my Grandma, and several friends. I suddenly changed jobs, which brought on grief from the distance it created with the friends that I had made. There were lots of changes. Not everything was bad, but it seems like that's what sticks in my mind the most. I was reading through the Bible, and I found another guy who faced loss and change in a year's time.

Genesis 8:13-22. "Noah was now 601 years old. On the first day of the new year, ten and a half months after the flood began, the floodwaters had almost dried up from the earth. Noah lifted back the covering of the boat and saw that the surface of the ground was drying. Two more months went by, and at last the earth was dry! Then God said to Noah, "Leave the boat, all of you—you and your wife, and your sons and their wives. Release all the animals— the birds, the livestock, and the small animals that scurry along the ground—so they can be fruitful and multiply throughout the earth." So Noah, his wife, and his sons and their wives left the boat. And all of the large and small animals and birds came out of the boat, pair by pair. Then Noah built an altar to the Lord, and there he sacrificed as burnt offerings the animals and birds that had been approved for that purpose. And the Lord was pleased with the aroma of the sacrifice and said to himself, 'I will never again curse the ground because of the human race, even though everything they think or imagine is bent toward evil from childhood. I will never again destroy all living things. As long as the earth remains, there will be planting and harvest, cold and heat, summer and winter, day and night.'"

Noah spent a little over a year experiencing hardship, probably worry and uncertainty. We know the story of how it rained for forty days and forty nights, but it took 11 months to dry up. I know that Noah was in a great relationship with God, but I think that he was still concerned about the future because when he opened that boat, the only living animals on earth would be with him. Where would they live? Their home was gone. Where were they? What would they find when they went out? There were lots of unknowns. Noah had also experienced loss. Think of the friends who laughed at him and who died. I wonder if he had any brothers and sisters who died during that flood. He had land and crops with livestock that were gone. I know that he and God were close, but he was human. I'm sure he had some thoughts and questions during that year. However, look at what it says in the end of the scriptures: God will not destroy all living things ever again.

That gives us hope and a certain amount of peace. Nowhere in the Bible does it say that we won't face hard times and loss. However, it says in many places that God will be with us. Just as He won't destroy the land again, He won't destroy us. When things get tough, remember that when God is with us, who is there to fear?

The thing about a new year is that we can have a new start on things. Just like when Noah stepped off the Ark, he started over completely. We can too. It's never too late. Not only do we have a chance to start new for the year; when we accept Jesus in our lives, we get to start new, clean, and clear, which promises us everlasting life. I want to challenge you to make your relationship with Jesus better this year than last. Happy New Year!

Find a Place to Pray

"And Satan trembles when he sees;
The weakest saint upon his knees."
– William Cowper

Growing up in the country and on a farm, we always had horses and cows. I liked riding horses, and I can certainly agree with Winston Churchill on this quote:

"There is something about the outside of a
horse that is good for the inside of a man."
– Winston Churchill

I can't ride anymore. I don't even own a horse now, but riding certainly gives you time with God. I also liked to go check cows. To see some of His creatures was very calming and gave me a time of prayer, but now I don't have any cows to check. It would seem as if I have lost my prayer time doesn't it. However, that's not true. I pray when I sit in a deer stand and even when I drive down the road. I have found that lots of people don't know that they can pray without being in church. That's not true. Nowhere in the Bible does it place a restriction on where we can pray. Joseph prayed in a dry well, and

Daniel prayed in a lion's den. It's not important where we pray but that we pray and that we do it with the right frame of mind.

Proverbs 15:8. "The Lord detests the sacrifice of the wicked, but he delights in the prayers of the upright."

So when we pray in an honest, humble manner, God is happy. When God is happy, good things happen.

Psalm 6:9. "The Lord has heard my plea; the Lord will answer my prayer. "

King David said that the Lord will answer his prayer, but I must warn you that what God gives is what we need, and very often, that is not what we "want."

Matthew 7:7-11. "Keep on asking, and you will receive what you ask for. Keep on seeking, and you will find. Keep on knocking, and the door will be opened to you. For everyone who asks, receives. Everyone who seeks, finds. And to everyone who knocks, the door will be opened. You parents—if your children ask for a loaf of bread, do you give them a stone instead? Or if they ask for a fish, do you give them a snake? Of course not! So if you sinful people know how to give good gifts to your children, how much more will your heavenly Father give good gifts to those who ask him?"

One thing that is hard for us is to wait for things. This is a test and a time to strengthen our faith in God. God will provide, but it's on His time. He's not late or early; God is always on time.

Romans 5:4. "And endurance develops strength of character, and character strengthens our confident hope of salvation."

When we are faithful in our walk with God and we trust Him, He will give us what we need. Again, notice that it doesn't say what we *want* but that all of our needs will be met.

2 Corinthians 9:8. "And God will generously provide all you need. Then you will always have everything you need and plenty left over to share with others."

I want to close with this story. It's one of my favorite stories in the Bible.

1 Kings 17:8-16. "Then the Lord said to Elijah, 'Go and live in the village of Zarephath, near the city of Sidon. I have instructed a widow there to feed you.' So he went to Zarephath. As he arrived at the gates of the village, he saw a widow gathering sticks, and he asked her, 'Would you please bring me a little water in a cup?' As she was going to get it, he called to her, 'Bring me a bite of bread, too.' But she said, 'I swear by the Lord your God that I don't have a single piece of bread in the house. And I have only a handful of flour left in the jar and a little cooking oil in the bottom of the jug. I was just gathering a few sticks to cook this last meal, and then my son and I will die.' But Elijah said to her, 'Don't be afraid! Go ahead and do just what you've said, but make a little bread for me first. Then use what's left to prepare a meal for yourself and your son. For this is what the Lord, the God of Israel, says: There will always be flour and olive oil left in your containers until the time when the Lord sends rain and the crops grow again!' So she did as Elijah said, and she and Elijah and her family continued to eat for many days. There was always enough flour and olive oil left in the containers, just as the Lord had promised through Elijah."

Prayer is the way to answered prayers. You don't have to pray in a certain place or a certain way. We just need to talk to Him [Jesus] like we talk to a loved one. When we do this and are faithful, our needs will be met. We might not become rich, but with strong prayer and solid faith, we can have wealth beyond measure.

Cornerstone

"Use missteps as stepping stones to deeper understanding and greater achievement."
– Susan Taylor

Being a farmer, I've spent a lot of time dealing with rocks. Sometimes rocks are good when you need to block a wheel or maybe use one as a hammer or to park a trailer jack on. Like Forrest Gump said, "Sometimes there just aren't enough rocks." Other times I have found myself picking up rocks to get them out of the pasture or the field because those things are rough on a sickle mower, and back in the day of the bar and chain hay balers, a rock in the hay could cause you to come to a stop until you straightened the bar. So many times, we throw rocks to the side, but they can and do play a large role in our lives.

Psalm 118:22. "The stone that the builders rejected has now become the cornerstone."

That man named Jesus, some people looked at Him like a rock when He was walking with man. To some, He was their piece of stability and hope, and to others, He was someone who was trying to destroy their lives because He preached that they needed to change. Eventually folks tried to cast Him to the side. To do this, they first nailed Jesus to the cross, and when His body had died, they buried Him behind a BIG Rock. It took several men to roll that stone in front of the tomb. Now, let me tell you how strong and how solid Jesus is. Many tried to kill Him, but they couldn't get it done. Then many men rolled a boulder in front of the tomb, but Jesus just told it to move. He told His friends what was going to happen, and He came back just like He said, even when others had cast Him away.

Friends, Jesus offers us eternal or never-ending life, but He does so much more. He has plans and blessings for us here in this life. All that He asks is that we make Him our cornerstone—our foundation. Life can be rough, but if we base it on the *Best Foundation* of Jesus, we can withstand any storm.

Mom

*"When God thought of mother, He must
have laughed with satisfaction, and framed it
quickly—so rich, so deep, so divine, so full of
soul, power, and beauty, was the conception."*
– Henry Ward Beecher

HAND THAT ROCKS THE CRADLE[4]
by Glen Campbell

There ought to be a hall of fame for mamas
Creation's most unique and precious pearls
And heaven help us always to remember
That the hand that rocks the cradle rules the
world

She taught him all the attributes of greatness
That she knew he couldn't learn away from
home
And by the time she wore the cover off her
bible
Her hair was gray and her little man was gone

One area of my life that has made a great
impression on me is the number of quality mothers I
have been around. In farming, family is very
important. The people who often hold it all together

---

[4] "Hand That Rocks the Cradle," Words and Music by Tedd Harris; from
the Album *Still Within the Sound of My Voice* (1987).

are Mom and Grandma; they are certainly special and a true gift from God.

As I have gotten older, I have gained a great respect for women and the role that a strong, Godly woman has in building the foundation for the world.

As Jimmy Dean says in the song *IOU*, ". . . And for cementin' together a family so it would stand the worst kinds of shocks and blows . . . and for layin' down a good strong foundation to build a life on."

When she builds a foundation for her family that can withstand the storms of life, a woman–a Mother–is actually laying the foundation for a better world. The neat thing is that this isn't a new concept; Solomon wrote about it long ago.

Proverbs 31:25-31. "She is clothed with strength and dignity, and she laughs without fear of the future. When she speaks, her words are wise, and she gives instructions with kindness. She carefully watches everything in her household and suffers nothing from laziness. Her children stand and bless her. Her husband praises her: 'There are many virtuous and capable women in the world, but you surpass them all!' Charm is deceptive, and beauty does not last; but a woman who fears the Lord will be greatly praised. Reward her for all she has done. Let her deeds publicly declare her praise."

As educators, we often talk about how important home life is for a child. The home builds an example for kids to follow, and mothers are the directors. As we read above, Solomon talks about how important the woman's role is and how women should be treated.

I love my Mother and, to tell you the truth, I've had a lot of "moms." These women took me in and helped make me a better person when my parents weren't around. Women who are "moms" or step into a mother's role when they are needed deserve a medal. They take on a task that they easily could have walked away from.

Now that I'm married, I still see these strong women who are wives, mothers, and leaders. They continue to set an example of how a Godly person, a family leader, and a parent should act. I learned long ago that when we have a chance to learn from someone who has a strong relationship with God, it is best to do it. Thank you, Moms, for being the example of what a Godly parent and leader should be.

The Misunderstood Farmer's Wife

*"A good marriage would be between
a blind wife and a deaf husband."*
– Honore De Balzac

Being married isn't easy. It takes work. We give up parts of ourselves to become one. In marriage, your cares become their cares, your troubles become their troubles, and your joys become their joys.

Genesis 2:24. "This explains why a man leaves his father and mother and is joined to his wife, and the two are united into one."

I want to look at a woman, a wife, and mother that we don't know a lot about. Really she is defined by 10 words or so. This woman is the wife of Job.

I entitled this *The Misunderstood Farmer's Wife* because that's what I feel that she is. Look at this passage . . .

Job 2:8-10. "Job scraped his skin with a piece of broken pottery as he sat among the ashes. His wife said to him, 'Are you still trying to maintain your integrity? Curse God and die.' But Job replied, 'You talk like a foolish woman. Should we accept only good things from the hand of God and never anything bad?' So in all this, Job said nothing wrong."

Now you might be thinking that she's pretty clear here. She probably doesn't care for Job or the problems that he is having. She seems so tired of him that she just wants him to die. Oh but my friend as Paul Harvey would say, "Now for the rest of the story." We know what happened to Job. God let Satan test him. In doing so, Job lost most everything, his cows, camels, all of his livestock, all of his crops, his servants, his kids, and even his health. Job did nothing wrong, so he couldn't figure out why this was happening, but even his best friends were telling him that he must have done something bad.

So where does Mrs. Job fit in to all of this? I don't know exactly how things went back in those days, but I know that Job was a farmer. I know that if the farmer has a wife, she, too, is a farmer. She probably spent some time milking that mean old cow that kicked the bucket over every time; and she probably helped harvest grain and cook meals. As I said, she was a farmer, too, so she would be upset. Then everyone felt bad for Job because he lost his kids. Who gave birth to the kids? That gives her rights to grieve. Then look back at what I said about marriage and the passage from Genesis. What hurts one, hurts the other. So we get to the point where she tells Job to curse God and die. Here are some reasons that I feel she did this, and none of them have anything to do with not loving Job.

Reason 1. She loved Job so much that she couldn't bear to see him suffer. Did she want him to leave? No, but she felt like it would be better for him. His pain would end.

Reason 2. She was mad with grief. What happens to one in a marriage happens to both. Oftentimes, it's harder on the one not directly affected. She lost her children; that alone would be terrible, but then she sees years of work gone in an instant.

Reason 3. Where was her support system? We see Job had friends (although not good friends) surrounding him. We don't know about her though. Did some of the other ladies come to be with her? We don't know. I bet she had to deal with questions like this too, "How's Job? Boy that was bad what happened to him. If he needs anything let us know." I wonder how many people asked how she was doing.

So let's fast forward to today. What can we learn from the misunderstood farmer's wife? There are lots of emotions that married people go through. When one is hurting, they both are hurting; so if someone in that relationship acts strange, remember that. Also, it is important to ask how they are doing. They might not be the one who is sick or depressed, but that doesn't mean they don't experience pain, worry, and doubt. They need our prayers just the same.

Remember that the farmer's wife is a farmer, too. By that, I mean they both have emotional attachments to things, because when they said "I do" they became one. So when you are comforting and praying for someone in a marriage who is in need, remember that person's "other half."

Mother Hen

"The hen's eyes are with her chickens."
– Unknown

I don't know how many of you have ever been around a mother hen, but she is very protective. She protects the eggs while she sits on them and uses her body heat to incubate them, then protects the chicks as she gets them big enough to take care of themselves. I've seen mother hens attack snakes and other predators that would be trying to harm the baby chicks. She is willing to risk her life for them. Sometimes during these events, her chicks get scattered. She will cluck and run around, trying to gather them up. Lots of times, we are like those chicks that get scattered. Jesus wants us back.

Matthew 23:37-39. "'O Jerusalem, Jerusalem, the city that kills the prophets and stones God's messengers! How often I have wanted to gather your children together as a hen protects her chicks beneath her wings, but you wouldn't let me. And now, look, your house is abandoned and desolate. For I tell you this, you will never see me again until you say, 'Blessings on the one who comes in the name of the Lord!'"

In this scripture, Jesus is talking to Jerusalem, but I really feel like He could be talking to all of us. There are many ways that we as a society have pushed God away and have discredited those who teach His Word. Then we wonder why it seems like He has abandoned us when we are the ones who walked toward the world and away from Him.

Jesus tells Jerusalem and us how to gather back together under Him like chicks under the wings of the mother hen. We must have faith in Him. Then we need to call on Him, telling Him our thoughts and fears and giving thanks. When we do that, we can experience the safety and secure feeling that only Jesus can provide.

I Love You Grandma

*"The simplest toy, one which even the
youngest child can operate, is called a
grandparent." – Sam Levenson*

My grandmother was great – plain and simple.
She was one of those people who loved everyone. No
matter who you were or where you were from, she
loved you. I guess like most grandmothers, she loved
all kids, but the love that she had for a pair of twin
boys – my brother and me – was something special.
From the baseball games in the backyard to jugs of
Kool-Aid®, she made sure to give us more than we
ever deserved. As I got older and I would cook, I'd
call her for recipes. No matter how close I followed
her directions, I could never make it taste the same. I
have since found that she added one ingredient that I
couldn't possibly add, and that ingredient was the
love of a grandmother. Her love extended much
further than the food. She instilled the unconditional
love of God to all whom she met.

2 Timothy 1:5-7. "I remember your true
faith. That kind of faith first belonged to your
grandmother Lois and to your mother Eunice. I know
you now have that same faith. That is why I want you
to remember the gift God gave you. God gave you

that gift when I laid my hands on you. Now I want you to use that gift and let it grow more and more, like a small flame grows into a fire. The Spirit God gave us does not make us afraid. His Spirit is a source of power and love and self-control."

My Grandmother was proud of all of her kids and grandkids in all that we did, but there was nothing that brought her greater joy than to watch us accept Christ and walk according to His will. She didn't say much about faith with her words, but her actions spoke volumes. She beat cancer twice, raised a family of those who were related by blood, and those related by love. In her 88 years, she fed a bunch of people and made tons of popcorn balls, and every minute was lived with unconditional love. I cry because I will miss you, but it is selfish of me to be sad because you left. You ran the good race. Congratulations, Grandma, enjoy eternal life in the glow of Jesus! I love you.

A Mother's Love

*"If you raise your children to feel that they
can accomplish any goal or task they decide
upon, you will have succeeded as a parent and
you will have given your children the greatest
of all blessings." – Brian Tracy*

I recently wrote a piece entitled *The Misunderstood Farmer's Wife*. I had a friend tell me that Lot's wife was misunderstood, too. The more I thought about my friend's statement and prayed about it, I felt that I needed to let Lot's wife teach a lesson, too. However, I'm not so sure that Lot's wife was misunderstood so much as she was conflicted and dealing with the impending loss of some of her children.

We don't know much about this woman. We don't even know her name. In the Bible, she was simply referred to as Lot's wife. What she dealt with was not unlike what parents today face; that is, the life choices of our children. For those who don't know the story, here it is:

Genesis 19:1-26. "That evening the two angels came to the entrance of the city of Sodom. Lot was sitting there, and when he saw them, he stood up to meet them. Then he welcomed them and bowed with his face to the ground. 'My lords,' he said, 'come

to my home to wash your feet, and be my guests for
the night. You may then get up early in the morning
and be on your way again.' 'Oh no,' they replied.
'We'll just spend the night out here in the city square.'
But Lot insisted, so at last they went home with him.
Lot prepared a feast for them, complete with fresh
bread made without yeast, and they ate. But before
they retired for the night, all the men of Sodom,
young and old, came from all over the city and
surrounded the house. They shouted to Lot, 'Where
are the men who came to spend the night with you?
Bring them out to us so we can have sex with them!'
So Lot stepped outside to talk to them, shutting the
door behind him. 'Please, my brothers,' he begged,
'don't do such a wicked thing. Look, I have two virgin
daughters. Let me bring them out to you, and you can
do with them as you wish. But please, leave these men
alone, for they are my guests and are under my
protection.' 'Stand back!' they shouted. 'This fellow
came to town as an outsider, and now he's acting like
our judge! We'll treat you far worse than those other
men!' And they lunged toward Lot to break down the
door. But the two angels reached out, pulled Lot into
the house, and bolted the door. Then they blinded all
the men, young and old, who were at the door of the
house, so they gave up trying to get inside.
Meanwhile, the angels questioned Lot. 'Do you have

any other relatives here in the city?' they asked. 'Get
them out of this place—your sons-in-law, sons,
daughters, or anyone else. For we are about to destroy
this city completely. The outcry against this place is so
great it has reached the Lord, and he has sent us to
destroy it.' So Lot rushed out to tell his daughters'
fiancés, 'Quick, get out of the city! The Lord is about
to destroy it.' But the young men thought he was only
joking. At dawn the next morning the angels became
insistent. 'Hurry,' they said to Lot. 'Take your wife
and your two daughters who are here. Get out right
now, or you will be swept away in the destruction of
the city!' When Lot still hesitated, the angels seized his
hand and the hands of his wife and two daughters and
rushed them to safety outside the city, for the Lord
was merciful. When they were safely out of the city,
one of the angels ordered, 'Run for your lives! And
don't look back or stop anywhere in the valley!
Escape to the mountains, or you will be swept away!'
'Oh no, my lord!' Lot begged. 'You have been so
gracious to me and saved my life, and you have
shown such great kindness. But I cannot go to the
mountains. Disaster would catch up to me there, and
I would soon die. See, there is a small village nearby.
Please let me go there instead; don't you see how
small it is? Then my life will be saved.' 'All right,' the
angel said, 'I will grant your request. I will not destroy

the little village. But hurry! Escape to it, for I can do nothing until you arrive there.' This explains why that village was known as Zoar, which means "little place." Lot reached the village just as the sun was rising over the horizon. Then the Lord rained down fire and burning sulfur from the sky on Sodom and Gomorrah. He utterly destroyed them, along with the other cities and villages of the plain, wiping out all the people and every bit of vegetation. But Lot's wife looked back as she was following behind him, and she turned into a pillar of salt."

The cities of Sodom and Gomorrah were very wicked places. That's why God was to destroy them. In these cities there were all kinds of sin, drinking, drugs, sex, you name it. That sounds a lot like our world today. God instructed Lot to warn his family that didn't live with him, but his warning fell on deaf ears. So when they were running from the destruction, Lot's wife looked back, I guess hoping to see her kids running behind them. When she did this, she disobeyed God, which is why I say she wasn't misunderstood. She knowingly went against a direct order from God. Several hundred years later, Jesus reminds people of this.

Luke 17:31-35. "On that day a person out on the deck of a roof must not go down into the house to pack. A person out in the field must not return home. Remember what happened to Lot's wife! If you cling to your life, you will lose it, and if you let your life go, you will save it. That night two people will be asleep in one bed; one will be taken, the other left. Two women will be grinding flour together at the mill; one will be taken, the other left."

Do I blame Lot's wife for loving her children? Absolutely not, but here are the lessons to be learned:

Lesson One. Several years ago, I would drive my Grandma home from church. One day, I said, "I bet you go to church just so I can drive you home." She said, "No, I love you, but I go to church for myself and no one else." She said that a person's relationship with God is one that has to be selfish. You can't go to church for someone else. You can pray for them and try to teach them, but in the end, each person has to build their own relationship with God. It doesn't matter if they are your father, mother, brother, sister, child, or grandchild; they have to make that decision on their own. While this is *one* of the most painful – if not *the most* painful – things we have to do as a parent, we can't let the love we have for our kids take us away from Jesus.

Lesson Two. Children, please try to understand the love that your parents have for you – whether they're your biological parents or not. We will do whatever we can to make your life work. So what is it going to hurt you to listen to the preacher? If you give God a chance, He wants to be in your life. He's hurting when you seek Him and His love, but please understand that if we don't follow His instructions, we will eventually turn to dust and be blown away from Him forever.

Author's Note

The remaining devotions in the book are the thoughts and feelings that God put on my heart in 2016. They cover a wide range of issues. You'll find devotions about love, grief, and marriage; Christmas and other holidays; doubt and how the enemy uses it to attack us. I believe that over the year, God covers most of our life experience. I hope that God speaks to you as you read these.

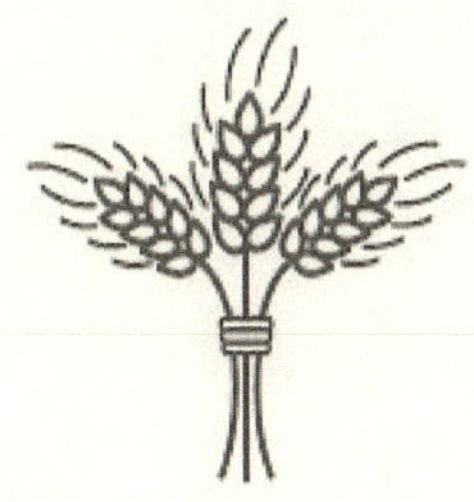

Reader's Notes

The Day the Town of
Guy, Arkansas, Wept

*"All I really, really want our love to do is to
bring out the best in me and in you too."*
— Joni Mitchell

Yesterday I had a relative pass away. Growing up in the small town that we did, it was easy to be close to the people around you. This man had an infectious smile and a laugh that you would never forget. Having moved away, I didn't get to visit with him a lot recently. When he became sick, I knew that he would fight. I would see him at church and ask how he was doing. His answer was the same every time. "Man I'm not doing real good, but God's got this, so I'm not worried." This guy knew where he was going. He knew it very well.

Jeremiah 29:11-13. "For I know the plans I have for you," says the Lord. "They are plans for good and not for disaster, to give you a future and a hope. In those days when you pray, I will listen. If you look for me wholeheartedly, you will find me."

So yesterday when I found out that he had passed away, I couldn't help but smile and think what a good race he had run. I know he is in a place that I cannot imagine how great it is.

Then I started to think about his family, his friends, our town, and all of the people who were touched by him. There was one story in the Bible that came to mind, and one verse stood out that I feel happened yesterday.

John 11:35. "Then Jesus wept."

You see, this verse is from a story of a man who had died. Jesus arrived and saw the reaction of the family, the friends, and town, and Jesus wept. I believe that Jesus wept because of the sympathy and hurt that He felt for the loved ones. Jesus wasn't sad because of the death, because He knew what was to come for Lazarus. He was sad because of the pain that those left behind were feeling.

Yesterday, I'm sure Jesus was there with the family, and He wept with them. Friends, that's what makes Jesus so great. He wants to have a relationship with each of us. He wants to be more than just a passing friend; He wants to be a close friend. It would be easy for Him to say not to be sad because of all the great things ahead. Jesus understands loss and grief. He wants us to turn to Him when we are sad and lost. He wants to hold us. He wants to comfort us. He wants to weep with us. Will you let Him?

What Embarrasses You?

*"Most things in life are moments of pleasure
and a lifetime of embarrassment; photography
is a moment of embarrassment and a lifetime
of pleasure." — Tony Benn*

I'm to a point where I think that I can no longer watch some college sports. It's not that I don't like them, it's that I am a passionate person about certain things. In college sports, we see a win-now-at-almost-any-cost mindset. I'm not like that. I'm okay with my team not winning sometimes, but I want them to lose in a respectful way. I see college sports as a training ground for tomorrow's leaders. I understand that winning makes the sports world "go round," but if we instill a sense of "as long as you win you can do what you want" mindset, we are setting our athletes up for future failure. I have seen lots of Facebook posts that say they are embarrassed to be an Arkansas Razorback because of a game that they blew a 24-point lead in. While I am not happy with that game's outcome, I am a long way from being embarrassed to be a Razorback. I am, however, embarrassed that I let others' words and opinions cause me to become upset. I certainly apologize for this, and I am trying to get better in this area of my life.

The reasons that I have for saying that I am not embarrassed are probably different than most, mainly because I don't let one area define my opinion of something. You see, I graduated from the University of Arkansas in 2004. My name is carved into a sidewalk on campus just like all the other U of A graduates. That university allowed me to travel across the country and meet some great people. The work that is done by Razorback students is changing the world. Now, you may be saying that these reasons are not sports-related. True; but the reason students come to college is to learn, including the athletes.

Proverbs 19:26. "Children who mistreat their father or chase away their mother are an embarrassment and a public disgrace."

I work with kids everyday who say that they are going to be pro athletes. When they tell me this, I am encouraging, but I ask questions such as, "what if you don't make it?" We count up how many players are in the league to see what competition is out there. Then we discuss the average length of a pro career, and they quickly realize that there are a lot more things to learn in life than just sports. I look at the program at the U of A, and from what I see, student athletes are held accountable for a lot of things; if they fall short, they lose their spot, which could hurt the team. Coaches could let it slide, but from what I see, they typically don't. I'm proud of that, not embarrassed at all.

Micah 7:16. "All the nations of the world will stand amazed at what the Lord will do for you. They will be embarrassed at their feeble power. They will cover their mouths in silent awe, deaf to everything around them."

Lastly, I want to address my reactions. I have to keep telling myself that it's just a game and that it's just others' opinions. I'm like many people who get their feelings hurt over something that won't matter at all tomorrow or next week. What I want to change in my life is that I don't get embarrassed and upset when I don't set a good example for others. I *want to be embarrassed* when I put foolish things like games over spending time with my family and with Jesus. I hope I'm embarrassed when I have the chance to teach right from wrong but choose not to. I also hope that I'm embarrassed if someone wants me to show them Jesus and I don't.

I'm disappointed that my team didn't win or that they aren't the best in all of the land, but to say that I am embarrassed by them, no I'm not. There are more important things in the world to be embarrassed about in life. When the game ends, we can walk away, hopefully learn from it, and play again. In life, we might only have one chance to tell someone about Jesus or to make our lives right, so if we fail at those, *then* we should be embarrassed, but not because of losing a game.

The Story of Old St. Nick

*"Authentic Christianity never destroys what
is good. It makes it grow, transfigures it,
and enriches itself from it." — Unknown*

I love Christmas. Growing up on a dairy farm, it was common that on Christmas Eve night, we would be out feeding and doing chores. I remember looking up at the night sky and wondering what those Shepherds must have thought, but I was also hoping to see Santa Claus. Many times, I've seen Facebook posts saying that we should not focus on Santa. Some say that we should even do away with the entire idea of Santa Claus. What if I told you that instead of diminishing Santa, we should be more like him? You might think that I have regressed in my walk with Jesus, but let me tell you a little story.

Many, many years ago, in about the third century in what is now southern Turkey, lived a man named Nickolas. He was raised to believe in God with all of his heart. He was so faithful that he was made a bishop in the church. When Nickolas's parents died, they left him a bunch of money. Well, being raised to follow Christ, he set out to help others both spiritually and financially. There are many stories about how he gave money to the poor, but one that stands out to me is one about a man who had three daughters. The time came for them to marry, but the man couldn't pay for weddings, and his daughters were about to be sold into slavery. Then one night, three sacks of money came through the window and landed in their shoes or stockings that were hung up to dry. There are many stories about this happening, and this is why kids hang up stockings to this day.

2 Corinthians 9:9-11. "As the Scriptures say, 'They share freely and give generously to the poor. Their good deeds will be remembered forever.' For God is the one who provides seed for the farmer and then bread to eat. In the same way, he will provide and increase your resources and then produce a great harvest of generosity in you. Yes, you will be enriched in every way so that you can always be generous. And when we take your gifts to those who need them, they will thank God."

Now I don't know where the elves and reindeer came from, but I do know that when Bishop Nickolas died, he became a saint and that through different translations of his name, we have Santa Claus.

The thing is, Santa started by following Jesus' directions to help those around us. In our fast-paced world, we often get so consumed with ourselves that Santa Claus becomes a story that we don't remember or believe in. It's important to remember the origin of Santa Claus, and if we will be more like Jesus, then Santa Claus will become real in the lives of those we touch.

Why Jesus Was Born in a Barn

"Love is the thing that enables a woman
to sing while she mops up the floor
after her husband has walked across it
in his barn boots." — Hoosier Farmer

One thing every farmer knows is that you will get dirty doing your job. I have never been in a barn with livestock where I didn't get a little of the atmosphere on me. On this day some 2,000 years ago, a child was born in a stable, and his bed was a manger. Mangers are dirty and dusty with bugs and livestock poop. It's no place for any baby, but this baby was the Child of God. Why would Jesus be born in a dirty, smelly stable?

Luke 2:7. "She gave birth to her firstborn son. She wrapped him snugly in strips of cloth and laid him in a manger, because there was no lodging available for them."

You see, in those stables were beasts of burden. Cows, camels, horses, and donkeys were housed there so that they could do a job, but they were replaceable. The people who tended to those animals were dirty and looked down upon, but it wasn't an accident that Jesus was born there. Jesus is spotless and free of sin and by being born there, Jesus showed that there is no place too low or dirty for Him to go to show His love.

Luke 2:8-14. "That night there were shepherds staying in the fields nearby, guarding their flocks of sheep. Suddenly, an angel of the Lord appeared among them, and the radiance of the Lord's glory surrounded them. They were terrified, but the angel reassured them. 'Don't be afraid!' he said. 'I bring you good news that will bring great joy to all people. The Savior—yes, the Messiah, the Lord—has been born today in Bethlehem, the city of David! And you will recognize him by this sign: You will find a baby wrapped snugly in strips of cloth, lying in a manger.' Suddenly, the angel was joined by a vast host of others—the armies of heaven—praising God and saying, 'Glory to God in highest heaven, and peace on earth to those with whom God is pleased.'"

The Shepherds of the time were often looked at as less than human. They were not respected or loved. When Jesus was born, the angels announced it, not to the kings and religious leaders, but to the poorest of the poor. Why did God do this? Because His love is for everyone – rich and poor.

John 3:16-17. "For this is how God loved the world: He gave his one and only Son, so that everyone who believes in him will not perish but have eternal life. God sent his Son into the world not to judge the world, but to save the world through him.

On this celebration of the day of His birth, let's remember why Jesus came. It wasn't for notoriety or fame but because He loves you and me. No matter what we do for a living or how much money we have, He came to pay for our sins. As we give gifts today, let us all remember the Gift that we received in a manger so long ago.

Grandma's Christmas Gifts

"A gift consists not in what is done or given,
but in the intention of the giver or doer."
— Seneca

In keeping with the theme of my last few pieces, I want to share one of my favorite Christmas memories. I remember as a kid, one of the gifts that my Grandma always gave was a paper sack that had an orange, an apple, and a candy cane. She said that when she was a little girl that gift was often all they got. I didn't understand at the time how such a small gift could mean so much. As I've grown, I see now that oftentimes it's not what the gift looks like, but it's the intent of the giver that determines the value.

John 4:7-14. "Soon a Samaritan woman came to draw water, and Jesus said to her, 'Please give me a drink.' He was alone at the time because his disciples had gone into the village to buy some food. The woman was surprised, for Jews refuse to have anything to do with Samaritans. She said to Jesus, 'You are a Jew, and I am a Samaritan woman. Why are you asking me for a drink?' Jesus replied, 'If you only knew the gift God has for you and who you are speaking to, you would ask me, and I would give you living water.' 'But sir, you don't have a rope or a bucket,' she said, 'and this well is very deep. Where would you get this living water? And besides, do you think you're greater than our ancestor Jacob, who gave us this well? How can you offer better water than he and his sons and his animals enjoyed?' Jesus replied, 'Anyone who drinks this water will soon become thirsty again. But those who drink the water I give will never be thirsty again. It becomes a fresh, bubbling spring within them, giving them eternal life.'"

Jesus uses the gift of a drink of water to prove a point. He said that soon after getting a drink of water from the well a person would become thirsty again; that drink a person got that was not given with love means nothing. But Jesus gave us all a gift of everlasting life. He didn't have to, but He did it because He loves us, which makes its value so high that we can't calculate it.

The gift that my Grandma gave was given to show that while the material value might not be much, her love for us made it invaluable. As we give gifts these next few days, I would encourage each of us, the giver and receiver, not to look at the gift by what it costs but by what it means. I hope that they are all given and received with love. That's the reason God sent Jesus into the world. He didn't look at the cost to determine the value.

A Tree for Christmas

*"Christmas is most truly Christmas when we
celebrate it by giving the light of love to those
who need it most." – Ruth Carter Stapleton*

One of the things I enjoy this time of year is
to sit with all of the lights off except the ones that are
on the Christmas tree. I like to look at the bright
lights in the darkness with the beautiful decorations.
This reminds me of God. Now I have seen on
Facebook where people talk about the tree not having
any real meaning of Christmas. I'm going to show you
that it does and why we might want to keep it up all
year long.

You see, many hundreds of years ago, a guy
named Boniface was out spreading the good news of
Jesus. He was in Germany where he met some folks
who worshipped a god that they thought was an oak
tree and that anyone who touched the tree would die.
To prove them wrong, one day Boniface chopped
down the old oak tree. When nothing happened to
him, the Germans started to listen to him. Then
Boniface pointed to an evergreen tree. He said that if
they wanted a tree to symbolize God that an
evergreen tree was it.

Revelation 1:8. "I am the Alpha and the Omega—the beginning and the end," says the Lord God. "I am the one who is, who always was, and who is still to come—the Almighty One."

Think about the Christmas tree in terms of this scripture. They normally have branches from the ground up. The trees true to the evergreen label are almost always green year around. Then just look at the shape. It points up to Heaven. When we decorate it with lights, this reminder of God shines light into the darkness. The ornaments represent the good news and grace that God provides. To drive home the point, we have an angel or star on top to point the way. An oak tree might be strong, but the leaves die in the fall; and when there is a storm the oak tree breaks, but the evergreen tree bends, but doesn't break as easily. Just like the Christmas tree, Jesus doesn't die or change. He can withstand any storm. He is the light in this dark world, and He wants to bless us. So when I think about it, I think we might benefit from having this reminder in front of us every day.

A Guest

*"A guest never forgets the host
who had treated him kindly." – Homer*

THE CHRISTMAS GUEST5
It happened one day near December's end
Two neighbors called on an old time friend
And they found his shop so meager and mean.
Made gay with a thousand bows of green

And Conrad was sittin' with face ashined.
When he suddenly stopped as he stiched a
twine
And he said "Oh friends at dawn today
When the cock was crowin' the night away

The Lord appeared in a dream to me
And said 'I'm comin' your guest to be.'
So I've been busy with feet astir
And strewin' my shop with branches of fir.

The table is spread and the kettle is shined
And over the rafters the holly is twined.
And now I'll wait for my Lord to appear
And listen closely so I will hear His step

As He nears my humble place
And I'll open the door and look on His face".
So his friends went home and left Conrad alone

---

[5] From the album Here Comes the Champion. Helen Steiner Rice wrote the lyrics to "The Christmas Guest," a sentimental song first performed by country music legend, Grandpa Jones back in 1963.

For this was the happiest day he'd known.

For long since his family had passed away
And Conrad had spent many a sad Christmas
day.
But he knew with the Lord as his Christmas
guest
This Christmas would be the dearest and best.

So he listened with only joy in his heart
And with every sound he would rise with a start
And look for the Lord to be at his door.
Like the vision he'd had a few hours before.

So he ran to the window after hearin' a sound
But all he could see on the snow-covered
ground
Was a shabby begger whose shoes were torn
And all of his clothes were ragged and worn.

But Conrad was touched and he went to the
door
And he said "your feet must be frozen and sore
I have some shoes in my shop for you
And a coat that'll keep you warmer too".

So with grateful heart, the man went away
But Conrad noticed the time of day
And he wondered what made the Lord so late.
And how much longer he'd have to wait.

When he heard a knock he ran to the door
But it was only a stranger once more.
A bent ol' lady with a shawl of black.

With a bundle of kindlin' piled on her back.

She asked for only a place to rest
But that was reserved for Conrad's great guest.
But her voice seemed to plead "Don't send me away,
Let me rest for a while on Christmas day".

So Conrad brewed her a steamin' cup
And told her to sit at the table and sup.
But after she left he was filled with dismay
For he saw that the hours were slippin' away

And the Lord hadn't come as He said He would
And Conrad felt sure he'd misunderstood.
When out of the stillness he heard a cry,
"Please help me, and tell me where am I!"

So again he opened his friendly door
And stood disappointed as twice before.
It was only a child who'd wandered away
And was lost from her family on Christmas Day.

Again, Conrad's heart was heavy and sad
But he knew he should make the little girl glad.
So he called her in and he wiped her tears
And quieted all her childish fears

Then he led her back to her home once more.
But as he entered his own darkened door
He knew that the Lord was not comin' today.
For the hours of Christmas had passed away.

So he went to his room and he knelt down to pray

And he said "Dear Lord, why did You delay?
What kept You from comin' to call on me?
For I wanted so much Your Face to see."

When soft in the silence, a voice he heard
"Lift up your head, for I kept my word.
Three times my shadow crossed your floor
And three times I came to your lonely door.

For I was the begger with bruised, cold feet,
And I was the woman you gave somethin' to
eat.
And I was the child on the homeless street.
Three times I knocked and three times I came in

And each time I found the warmth of a friend.
Of all the gifts love is the best
And I was honored to be your Christmas guest."
– Grandpa Jones

I love this song. It's a great reminder of how Jesus interacts with us daily. The last two pieces that I have written have been about Christmas Trees and Santa. I wanted to show how the love of Jesus can be demonstrated in a lot of our Christmas traditions. However, it doesn't have to be Christmas for us to experience God or show others the greatness of God. It does seem like we think more about kindness and love in December . . . more than we do in the summer. Why is this?

Luke 19:5-10. "When Jesus came by, he looked up at Zacchaeus and called him by name.

'Zacchaeus!' he said. 'Quick, come down! I must be a guest in your home today.' Zacchaeus quickly climbed down and took Jesus to his house in great excitement and joy. But the people were displeased. 'He has gone to be the guest of a notorious sinner,' they grumbled. Meanwhile, Zacchaeus stood before the Lord and said, 'I will give half my wealth to the poor, Lord, and if I have cheated people on their taxes, I will give them back four times as much!' Jesus responded, 'Salvation has come to this home today, for this man has shown himself to be a true son of Abraham. For the Son of Man came to seek and save those who are lost.'"

The last sentence says, "For the Son of Man came to seek and save those who are lost." While it is awesome that we have programs to help others during Christmas, what about the other 11 months? I've heard it said that Christmas is the season for giving. I love it, but Jesus didn't have a season for saving the lost. So why don't we put out that kind of love and giving all year long?

Do I think if we all did this it would change the world? It could; but I know that if our actions help one person to have a relationship with Jesus, it will change their world.

Jesus gives us the gift of everlasting life because He loves us. I challenge us all to be like Jesus

and give as He gives! I challenge us all to make
Christmas a way of life, not just a time of year!

Never Ending Love in Marriage

*"Don't marry the person you think you can
live with; marry only the individual you
think you can't live without."*
– Dr. James C. Dobson

Yesterday was an amazing day. I was in a
small country church in Webb City, Oklahoma. It was
cold, windy, and blowing snow, but on the inside was
the warmth and celebration of a lifelong love. My
mother and father-in-law were married in December,
1966. We were having cake and punch, listening to
stories about 50 years of life. There were laughs and
tears, stories of good times and bad, but in each one
there was love and dedication.

Hebrews 13:4. "Give honor to marriage, and
remain faithful to one another in marriage. God will
surely judge people who are immoral and those who
commit adultery."

Paul wrote this simple scripture. He didn't say
that the married couple were to like each other all of
the time. I'm sure that in those 50 years my in-laws
had times when they didn't like what the other was
doing, but they always loved each other and never
gave up when times get tough.

Revelation 19:7-9. "Let us be glad and
rejoice, and let us give honor to him. For the time has

come for the wedding feast of the Lamb, and his bride has prepared herself. She has been given the finest of pure white linen to wear. For the fine linen represents the good deeds of God's holy people. And the angel said to me, 'Write this: Blessed are those who are invited to the wedding feast of the Lamb.' And he added, 'These are true words that come from God.'"

I have had the honor of having parents who have been married nearly 40 years, my grandparents on my dad's side were married nearly 50 years and my grandparents on my mom's side were married over 50 years. These people gave a good example of how we should try to live, but also they are the living example of how God loves us. When we read what John wrote in Revelation, "We are the bride that The Lamb (Jesus) is preparing to wed." In all of this time, I know there are many things in this world that God doesn't like, but through it all, He still loves us and is committed to being in relationship with us.

To my in-laws, congratulations on the milestone, and along with my parents, thank you for being an example of what God's love in marriage should look like.

The Greatest Gift that God Gave to Husbands and Wives

*"My wife is a sex object — every time I ask
for sex, she objects." — Les Dawson*

Sometimes I find myself in situations that make me scratch my head. I know that I normally don't write things that are touchy-feely or controversial, but I feel like the Lord laid this on me. I want to be clear about this devotional, IT DEALS WITH MARRIED COUPLES ONLY, NOT WITH PREMARITAL ACTIONS.

The other day I was in a discussion about some of the ways that Satan tries to destroy us and drive a wedge between us and God. Well it didn't take long for the conversation to turn to sex. The person leading the conversation said that a study showed that men think about sex 19 times a day while women think about it only 10 times a day. One lady in the group said she felt like the number was too low for men and too high for women. She went on to say that for her it might only be once or twice a day, if that much. This got me to thinking.

We know that pornography can cause us to become addicted to sex and lose the value of this gift God gave us. But, what if we go to the other extreme, where we're so busy – or worse, so self-absorbed – that we lose that intimate relationship, that fire of desire for our mate, the one God made for us?

Song of Solomon 2:2, 14, 16-17. "Like a lily among thistles is my darling among young women.

My dove is hiding behind the rocks, behind an outcrop on the cliff. Let me see your face; let me hear your voice. For your voice is pleasant, and your face is lovely.

My lover is mine, and I am his. He browses among the lilies. Before the dawn breezes blow and the night shadows flee, return to me, my love, like a gazelle or a young stag on the rugged mountains."

I went a little Old Testament there, but I want us to look at how Solomon describes the one that he loves and how she describes him. Now I know that this was probably a new love, but does that mean this type of feeling is meant to go away? I know that sometimes it does, but is it because we let that feeling go away, and do we want to get it back?

The Apostle Paul never married, and he goes as far as to say that he thinks it would be best if everyone was single and focused on the Lord, but look at what he says in these scriptures.

1 Corinthians 7:2-5. "But because there is so much sexual immorality, each man should have his own wife, and each woman should have her own husband. The husband should fulfill his wife's sexual needs, and the wife should fulfill her husband's needs. The wife gives authority over her body to her husband, and the husband gives authority over his body to his wife. Do not deprive each other of sexual relations, unless you both agree to refrain from sexual intimacy for a limited time so you can give yourselves more completely to prayer. Afterward, you should come together again so that Satan won't be able to tempt you because of your lack of self-control."

Don't deprive each other of needs; it happens! It happened in my first marriage. We see it happen when one is upset with the other or as a way to get what we want. In reality, Satan is using feelings and ideas to drive a wedge in our relationship with each other. If Satan stays at it long enough, it may drive us to sin. This sin doesn't have to be adultery; it could be hard feelings and hate, along with doubt.

One of the most important things I have learned is to communicate, not only with each other but with ourselves and with God. If we find ourselves not having the same thoughts or feelings that we did at one time for our spouse, and it feels like a wedge is in between us, we need to ask ourselves why. Then we need to talk to our mate and pray to the Lord to guide us back so that we can enjoy the physical and emotional gifts of the one that He created for us.

How to Wash Away Sin

"It will all come out in the soap-suds."
– Unknown

I have been thinking about how it feels to work all day and be dirty. I remember when I was farming, I would come in and wash the dirt out of my hair and my clothes. Some of the clothes I had would be stained. Cow manure is hard to get out sometimes. Just like decisions and choices can leave a stain on our lives. In the following verse, we'll see what Jeremiah says to Israel:

Jeremiah 2:21-22. "But I was the one who planted you, choosing a vine of the purest stock—the very best. How did you grow into this corrupt wild vine? No amount of soap or lye can make you clean. I still see the stain of your guilt. I, the Sovereign Lord, have spoken!"

No matter how well we think we can hide something, God sees it. No matter how we spin it or what we tell ourselves, it still leaves a stain. When my old work shirt would get really stained, I would throw it away. Are we like that old rag? Does The Lord want to cast us aside? No, He doesn't. He wants us to take a bath. You see, unlike an old, stained shirt, we can be made clean and our stains removed— not by using soap but by using the blood of The Son.

Hebrews 10:22. "Let us go right into the presence of God with sincere hearts fully trusting Him. For our guilty consciences have been sprinkled with Christ's blood to make us clean, and our bodies have been washed with pure water."

The blood of Jesus can wash out stains that have been set in for years. We just have to ask Him to come in and wash us.

Thanksgiving Thankfulness

*"Not what we say about our blessings, but
how we use them, is the true measure of our
thanksgiving." – W. T. Purkiser*

Tomorrow is Thanksgiving, and a lot of memories are flooding my mind. For many years I would go to my grandma's house with my mom and dad. We would have the normal turkey and ham with more sides than we knew what to do with. Along with my parents, my uncles would be there and whoever else might drop by. At a young age I thought it was about the food, but as I got older I realized it was about family, love, and blessings.

This year I'm not there and neither are my grandma and one uncle; they will be dining with Jesus tomorrow (I always said that her dressing was heavenly). This year has been difficult for me. However, the lessons from thanksgivings past are reminding me of what we should do.

Psalm 100:4-5. "Enter his gates with thanksgiving; go into his courts with praise. Give thanks to him and praise his name. For the Lord is good. His unfailing love continues forever, and his faithfulness continues to each generation."

I said that this year has been tough for me but each time I think about it, I realize all of the great things that have happened in my life and in this past year. No matter how rough the road, God has always been there.

Revelation 7:11-12. "And all the angels were standing around the throne and around the elders and the four living beings. And they fell before the throne with their faces to the ground and worshipped God. They sang, 'Amen! Blessing and glory and wisdom and thanksgiving and honor and power and strength belong to our God forever and ever! Amen.'"

Tomorrow as we eat a lot and fellowship, please do so with thanksgiving in your heart. There are those who don't have family, friends, or food. Also if God gives us tomorrow, it will be a gift. Be grateful for it.

Don't Let the Cat Get Your Tongue

*"If you think nobody cares if you're alive, try
missing a couple of car payments."
– Earl Wilson*

I post a lot of different things to social media.
I'm proud of my family. I'm proud of my experience
in agriculture. I'm proud of my country. And I am
proud that God loves me. I often post several
pictures and statuses about all of these things. My
family posts normally get several likes. The farm and
USA posts are kind of hit or miss, and normally my
posts about God get a like or two and maybe a
comment, but not like the other posts. So, me being
me, I posted a picture of a cat that said, "I got a cat, I
had to swerve but I got it." I didn't add a caption I
just put it out there. Two days later, this picture has
gotten 43 total reactions; 23 were likes, 13 were
laughs, 5 were angry faces, 1 was a shocked face, and
1 was a sad face. There were comments by
14 different people, and 10 people were kind of
scolding me.

I learned several things with this post:

1. Lots of people like cats.
2. It doesn't say that I harmed the cat; it said
    I swerved and I got it. While it implies

one thing, people make that conclusion on their own.

3. Some people know me pretty well.

Maybe I should have calmed the drama by explaining why I posted this, but I really wanted honest reactions. I thought a lot about that when I received a message stating that I should, but then I thought about the discussion that Adam and God had about eating from the forbidden tree. If God truly had explained what would happen, then things might have been different, but look at what God says: **Genesis 2:15-17.** "The Lord God placed the man in the Garden of Eden to tend and watch over it. But the Lord God warned him, 'You may freely eat the fruit of every tree in the garden—except the tree of the knowledge of good and evil. If you eat its fruit, you are sure to die.'"

I have had many conversations with people about this type of thing. I get a variety of reasons why they speak up for animals, politics, or whatever, and why they *don't* speak up for God. One person said, "I don't want to hurt people's feelings by talking about God." Another person was talking about praying when eating in public and said, "I don't want to offend those around me or make others feel uncomfortable." If you come to my house or go out to eat with me, I am going to pray. I don't do it to look cool, I do it to thank God. That's my relationship with Him. I wonder if that's why some people don't like to comment on or share posts about God, because they are afraid that they might not look cool or that by telling the truth they will hurt people's feelings? I want to show you something Jesus said:

Matthew 10:32-33. "Everyone who acknowledges me publicly here on earth, I will also acknowledge before my Father in heaven. But everyone who denies me here on earth, I will also deny before my Father in heaven."

Paul tells this to Timothy:

2 Timothy 2:11-13. "This is a trustworthy saying: If we die with him, we will also live with him. If we endure hardship, we will reign with him. If we deny him, he will deny us. If we are unfaithful, he remains faithful, for he cannot deny who he is."

So how are you going to explain to Jesus that you got upset about a dog or horse or whatever but you really wanted to worship quietly because you might offend someone. I don't want to face Jesus after that because I'll show you what can happen when we do that in just a bit.

John 3:13-21. "No one has ever gone to heaven and returned. But the Son of Man has come down from heaven. And as Moses lifted up the bronze snake on a pole in the wilderness, so the Son of Man must be lifted up, so that everyone who believes in him will have eternal life. 'For this is how God loved the world: He gave his one and only Son, so that everyone who believes in him will not perish but have eternal life. God sent his Son into the world not to judge the world, but to save the world through him. There is no judgment against anyone who believes in him. But anyone who does not believe in him has already been judged for not believing in God's one and only Son. And the judgment is based on this fact: God's light came into the world, but people loved the darkness more than the light, for their actions were evil. All who do evil hate the light and refuse to go near it for fear their sins will be exposed. But those who do what is right come to the light so others can see that they are doing what God wants."

This is one of the most widely known passages in the Bible. I don't know how many people understand the power and love that is shown here. A perfect person who was in a perfect place came here to die so that we can live life eternal, but we don't want to talk about it because it might offend someone? We get upset about a cat or cow but not about following God's word?

Now I'm not saying that you have to like everything I write or everything that your preacher says, but why would you not want to share how much God means? Does He mean more to you than a cat? I hope so.

I said a few lines ago that I would show you what can happen if Jesus denies us before the Father. (I'll be honest, when I read Revelation I sometimes get like "Red Skelton, Jr., the mean widdle kid," and I scare myself.)

Revelation 20:11-15. "And I saw a great white throne and the one sitting on it. The earth and sky fled from his presence, but they found no place to hide. I saw the dead, both great and small, standing before God's throne. And the books were opened, including the Book of Life. And the dead were judged according to what they had done, as recorded in the books. The sea gave up its dead, and death and the grave gave up their dead. And all were judged according to their deeds. Then death and the grave were thrown into the lake of fire. This lake of fire is the second death. And anyone whose name was not found recorded in the Book of Life was thrown into the lake of fire."

John says that those whose names are not in the Book of Life will experience the second death by being thrown into the lake of fire. That's a horrible way to spend eternity. Please don't spend eternity separated from God because the cat got your tongue.

Hate is Like a Cancer

"Hatred is the coward's revenge for being intimidated." – George Bernard Shaw

In my line of work, I deal with emotions and thoughts. I often work with people who struggle with negative emotions, such as hate and holding a grudge. I have believed for years that hate is something much worse than cancer because the only real cure comes from inside us. I try to explain this to the young people I work with, but it wouldn't hold much water if I didn't practice what I preach.

Mark 11:24-25. "I tell you, you can pray for anything, and if you believe that you've received it, it will be yours. But when you are praying, first forgive anyone you are holding a grudge against, so that your Father in heaven will forgive your sins, too."

The past few weeks have been a roller coaster of thoughts and emotions for me. The other day I spoke to a man with whom I have had a difference of opinion. He said he hoped that I didn't have any hard feelings for him. At that moment, I was reminded of what I try to teach my students. This same man and I also attended the same church at one time, and I was reminded of what Pastor Rick had said: "It's not important how you arrive at a place, but it is important how you leave." He also said that holding hate and hard feelings is like drinking poison and expecting the other person to get sick.

I'm not sure what my face was saying, but I quoted my pastor to this man. I was reminded also of the scripture from Mark. If we want to be forgiven and have God not hold a grudge against us, we must forgive those who have wronged or hurt us.

I look at the quote that I started with, one thing that I don't think people can ever say about me is that I am a coward, but it isn't because I'm not intimidated, it's because I'm forgiven.

Romans 12:20-21. "Instead, 'If your enemies are hungry, feed them. If they are thirsty, give them something to drink. In doing this, you will heap burning coals of shame on their heads.' Don't let evil conquer you, but conquer evil by doing good."

While I like the part where being nice will be like heaping hot coals of shame on people who wrong us, I do hope that maybe they learn how to treat people better. But doing something just to show someone up isn't Christ-like to me, and it doesn't build character.

We all face, have faced, or will face situations where we might be tempted to hold some hate or hard feelings toward others, but I want you to remember that all of these are opportunities to grow

closer to God and let His light shine through us. I
encourage each of us to let go of those hard feelings
and forgive others because God let go of hard
feelings that He could have had for us; God
forgives us.

The Motivation of Fear

"Always do what you are afraid to do."
– Ralph Waldo Emerson

Sometimes I find it hard to write about things that hit me close to home. I wrestled with this for a week.

It seems strange to some people and even to myself at times that I fear things. I've had more surgeries than I can count, been in some good wrecks, been run over by bulls, fallen out of an announcers stand, and I spent five years working at a prison, yet today I still find myself battling fear. The thing about fear is that it might be of big things like storms or bears, or it could be little things, like bugs. For me the biggest fear that I have is the fear of failure. What if I can't do something or what if a business or hobby goes wrong? What if I fail; what will people think? What will my wife think? Will she still love me? I know that these fears might sound crazy, but be honest . . . what kinds of fears do you have?

1 John 4:16-18. "We know how much God loves us, and we have put our trust in his love. God is love, and all who live in love live in God, and God lives in them. And as we live in God, our love grows more perfect. So we will not be afraid on the day of judgement, but we can face him with confidence because we live like Jesus here in this world. Such love has no fear, because perfect love expels all fear. If we are afraid, it is for fear of punishment, and this shows that we have not fully experienced his perfect love."

The words fear and fearsome are mentioned in the Bible about 330 times. I've read most of the scriptures. Every one of them talked about overcoming fear. In the passage it tells us that Jesus gave us His love to remove fear from our lives and that the more we live like Him, the less fear we have. It goes on to say that if we still have fear of something it's because we have work still to do to receive His perfect love.

Jesus knows that we are a long way from perfect and that we will never be able to get there here on earth. That's why He gives us grace, mercy, and forgiveness. That doesn't mean we should stop trying to reach the understanding of perfect love; on the contrary, we should use His mercy, grace, and forgiveness to keep fighting off doubt and walk closer with Him.

Chin up buttercup! God's got this; let's trust Him and see what happens.

Jealousy

The other day I shared a post on Facebook about thanking a farmer. A man I don't know commented that he would thank real farmers not corporate scam farmers. I have stewed on this for a day or so, and now here are my thoughts. Well over 90% of American farms are family owned. I grew up on a family farm. I also spent almost eight years working on "corporate farms." I can tell you that—at least the guys I worked with—treat it a lot like a family farm. I'm not sure what this man has against large farms, but if you ask a community, they don't care who exactly owns it. They care that this farm spends money in town at the grocery stores, the farm store, and the café, and that the employees' kids go to the local school. Big farms also bring in jobs for other businesses. Some people just don't like the big farms that they consider to be "factory farms." I want you to know that all farms are factories; some are just bigger than others. Some people don't like big farms because they have a jaded view of what farming is. I had a guy tell me we should farm the way they did in the 50's through the 70's. I told him we would have to tear down houses and plow up shopping malls and golf courses to even be half way to the production needs. Still I have found another reason some people don't like big farms. It's because they are jealous. Someone has gotten something that they don't have, and they don't like to see success. We see this in personal life; I have even seen it between churches.

Many times people will use this jealousy as motivation to do something. While it may seem good to be working towards something, I want you to think about what motivates us. If we use revenge, envy, jealousy, or other negative emotions, we will never be satisfied. We will still have a hole to fill.

Ecclesiastes 4:4. "Then I observed that most people are motivated to success because they envy their neighbors. But this, too, is meaningless—like chasing the wind."

Sure I would love to have a big farm, but I don't. That doesn't mean that I am going to wish bad things on those who do. We have to realize that the best motivation is the Lord's Will. That is the only way to have true happiness. When we seek His Will; He will give us the best. It might not be what we think we want, but when we live up to God's plan for us, we will be able to fill that hole and be complete.

God's Word Is His Bond

"Fear is a noose that binds until it
strangles." – Jean Toomer

In society today, we have gotten to the point
where almost everything we do has to be finalized
with a written contract to make our agreement
binding. I guess that I have been lucky though;
through all of my years of announcing rodeos, I have
signed four contracts. I still feel like my word is good
enough. There was a time when our word was the
only thing we needed. Our integrity and honesty
defined us.

We have been given a promise by God. When
He says something, He means it. I find that I question
myself at times because God has made a promise to
me; however, I still doubt Him even though His word
is binding, and He can't lie.

Hebrews 6:13-19. "For example, there was
God's promise to Abraham. Since there was no one
greater to swear by, God took an oath in his own
name, saying: 'I will certainly bless you, and I will
multiply your descendants beyond number.' Then
Abraham waited patiently, and he received what God
had promised. Now when people take an oath, they
call on someone greater than themselves to hold them

to it. And without any question, that oath is binding. God also bound himself with an oath, so that those who received the promise could be perfectly sure that he would never change his mind. So God has given both his promise and his oath. These two things are unchangeable because it is impossible for God to lie. Therefore, we who have fled to him for refuge can have great confidence as we hold to the hope that lies before us. This hope is a strong and trustworthy anchor for our souls. It leads us through the curtain into God's inner sanctuary."

The enemy is going to try to trick us into thinking that God might back out on His word and promises. The enemy might also try to convince us that we might have misunderstood what God has told us. But let me make this clear: it is only a trick. When God told us this, His word was binding and true.

Jeremiah 29:11. "For I know the plans I have for you," says the Lord. "They are plans for good and not for disaster, to give you a future and a hope."

It might not be what we have in mind, but His way is worlds better than ours. We know that He loves us. How do know this? By the following passage:

John 3:15-17. "So that everyone who believes in him will have eternal life. 'For this is how God loved the world: He gave his one and only Son, so that everyone who believes in him will not perish but have eternal life.' God sent his Son into the world not to judge the world, but to save the world through him."

He sent Jesus to die. Jesus was tortured and killed for you and me. If God was going to lie to us or even change His mind, do you think that He would have put Jesus through all of this? I don't think so!!

At times it might be hard to trust our fellow man, but God never changes or goes back on His word. It would be nice if we could make our agreements as binding as His.

Weeds of Life

*"A weed is no more than a flower in
disguise, which is seen through at once, if love
give a man eyes." – James Russell Lowell*

I was in Wisconsin about nine years ago, and I
learned a lesson about weeds. A weed is a crop or a
plant that grows where you don't want it. On my tour
of farms in Wisconsin, alfalfa was considered both a
crop and a weed, depending on where it was
growing—in the lawn, it was a weed; over in the
pasture, it was a crop. They considered it a weed in
the lawn because it choked out the grass they were
trying to grow. It robbed water and nutrients from
the desired plants. In the pasture, where it had a use,
it was well liked.

Hosea 10:11-13. "Israel is like a trained heifer
treading out the grain—an easy job she loves. But I
will put a heavy yoke on her tender neck. I will force
Judah to pull the plow and Israel to break up the hard
ground. I said, 'Plant the good seeds of righteousness,
and you will harvest a crop of love. Plow up the hard
ground of your hearts, for now is the time to seek the
Lord, that he may come and shower righteousness
upon you.' But you have cultivated wickedness and
harvested a thriving crop of sins. You have eaten the

fruit of lies—trusting in your military might, believing that great armies could make your nation safe."

We all have weeds growing in us. Some of those weeds might be like the alfalfa in Wisconsin, where it does have a good use but gets going in the wrong place, or it could be a weed like pigweed, which I have found no good use for. All pigweed does is kill out everything around it.

Do we have both of these in us? Yes we do. I won't list any because I might leave some out. So what do we need to do to become weed-free? Well in farming, oftentimes we hire a consultant to help us inventory what we have and to help us develop a plan to better our operation. In our lives, we can get a consultant to help us, and He has even paid the bill for us. His name is Jesus. I would encourage each of us to spend time talking with Him. Have Him inventory your life, and follow His plan to better your operation.

Our Words Can Hurt

"Don't abuse your friends and expect
them to consider it criticism."
– Edgar Watson Howe

As I have gotten older, I have become more mindful of the words that I use. I struggle at times to be truthful and not derogatory. I mean it's hard. Then I find myself thinking that people just need to have thicker skin. As I thought about this today, I came to a conclusion that both sides are true, and if we could all work together in not being overly sensitive, while at the same time trying not to be or say things that might hurt somcone, I think we'd all be better off.

Ephesians 4:29. "Don't use foul or abusive language. Let everything you say be good and helpful, so that your words will be an encouragement to those who hear them."

In education, we tell students that there are no stupid questions. Even if my students ask one, I try to explain to them to stay on task but still not tell them that they asked a stupid question.

You never know when the enemy is going to try to use a comment to cause a person to doubt themselves and their worth. I posted a picture on my Facebook page that had a bowl of beans and a piece of cornbread with a question, "Does cornbread go with beans?" I love beans and cornbread and, apparently, so do most of the fifty people who commented and the two hundred who liked it, but would you believe that there were comments like, "What a stupid question," "Too stupid to answer," and just plain "Stupid"? I guess that those people think that beans and cornbread go so well together that there is no question. However, if you ask my wife and youngest daughter that same question, they would have a different answer.

My question is "Why?" Why would we want to help the enemy? Some things may seem very small to us, but to someone else, it could be huge. When we help Satan, we are helping drive a wedge in someone's relationship with God. Why would we do that? I think this might explain it:

Matthew 4:1. "Then Jesus was led by the Spirit into the wilderness to be tempted there by the devil."

The devil tempted Jesus so he is surely going to try to tempt us. He tempts us in many ways, but if he can set it up to where we hurt each other's walk with God, then the devil is ecstatic. That's why I am trying to be mindful of what I say. I'm a work in progress. I challenge all of us not to be an unknowing tool with our words in the devil's work.

Hope and Faith

"A man with a grain of faith in God never
loses hope, because he ever believes in the
ultimate triumph of Truth."
— Mahatma Gandhi

I've written a lot of things in my life. Some
have been funny, some have been inspirational, and at
times, some have been instructional. Those are my
least favorite. Why? Because it seems that I often had
to leave out one important part. To me, for anything
to work, you first have to have hope and faith. When
you write instructions, hope and faith seem to get left
out.

Galatians 3:2-5. "Tell me this one thing:
How did you receive the Spirit? Did you receive the
Spirit by following the law? No, you received the
Spirit because you heard the message about Jesus and
believed it. You began your life in Christ with the
Spirit. Now do you try to complete it by your own
power? That is foolish. You have experienced many
things. Were all those experiences wasted? I hope
they were not wasted! Does God give you the Spirit
because you follow the law? Does God work miracles
among you because you follow the law? No, God
gives you his Spirit and works miracles among you

because you heard the message about Jesus and believed it."

As farmers, we often have to use expensive products, and we don't get immediate results. When you plant a field, you first add the fertilizer, then the seed, and then you wait. If it's available, you fire up an electric well or a power unit, and you water the crop. You weed spray it and maybe add some more fertilizer. You start this process and wait for four months to see how well it paid off, if at all. The farmer uses recommend practices, but I can tell you if they don't have faith and hope in what they are doing, their crop will not produce. Sometimes we might even use a consultant, but again, if the farmer doesn't have faith and hope in the consultant, they probably won't see much return.

Life with God is like being a farmer. There are many publications and even more people around to tell you exactly what steps to take, what words to say, and what things to do. You can do it all, but if you don't have faith and hope in Him you probably aren't going to grow. God also puts helpers in our lives. These might be doctors, preachers, teachers or maybe just a friend, but if we don't have faith and hope in them that God wants what's best for us and that He wants to use these people to help us, then we will likely fail.

In everything that we do, we must pray and believe in the God that we pray to. When we have that faith, we will grow in amazing ways.

What Is Normal???

"Normal is a setting on a washing machine."

from
The Love We Share Without Knowing,
by Christopher Barzak

I shared a quote very similar to this one with a friend today, and he challenged me to write something about it. Here it is. I call it "Normal Is Deadly." This will go with my next writing about moving on to create a "new normal."

We hear the word *normal* used a lot, but what is "normal"? Regular? Average? Those may be some of the words we think of when the word *normal* is used. The problem is that in order to have a "normal," you must first have something to measure it against. We might be able to measure normal rainfall or normal temperature, but to try to say a "normal life" or a "normal person" is impossible, and trying to live that way can be deadly.

Exodus 14:21-31. "Moses raised his hand over the Red Sea, and the Lord caused a strong wind to blow from the east. The wind blew all night long. The sea split, and the wind made the ground dry. The Israelites went through the sea on dry land. The water was like a wall on their right and on their left. Then all of Pharaoh's chariots and horse soldiers followed them into the sea. Early that morning the Lord looked down from the tall cloud and column of fire at the Egyptian army. Then he made them panic. The wheels of the chariots became stuck. It was very hard to control the chariots. The Egyptians shouted, 'Let's get out of here! The Lord is fighting against us. He is fighting for the Israelites.' Then the Lord told Moses, 'Raise your hand over the sea to make the water fall and cover the Egyptian chariots and horse soldiers.' So just before daylight, Moses raised his hand over the sea. And the water rushed back to its proper level. The Egyptians were running as fast as they could from the water, but the Lord swept them away with the sea. The water returned to its normal level and covered the chariots and horse soldiers. Pharaoh's army had been chasing the Israelites, but that army was destroyed. None of them survived! But the Israelites crossed the sea on dry land. The water was like a wall on their right and on their left. So that day the Lord saved the Israelites from the Egyptians. Later, the Israelites saw the dead bodies of the Egyptians on the shore of the Red Sea. The Israelites saw the great power of the Lord when he defeated the Egyptians. So the people feared and respected the Lord, and they began to trust the Lord and his servant Moses."

In this passage, it tells what happened when the water returned to normal. Everyone in its way died. You might be thinking you don't have much to worry about because an army isn't chasing you across a sea, God isn't parting the water, and you won't get stuck in the mud and drown. You might be correct, but how many times do we face a monumental change in life? A time where we are being forced to move on? It happens often if we think about it . . . A new job. A death in the family. A graduation. One of the questions most often asked is "Can we just get back to normal?" It might sound good, but as we saw in the scriptures above, when some things return to normal, they die; so they never truly return, do they?

Each of us is unique; God created us that way. So to say that a person isn't normal cannot be confirmed. God's plan for our lives is as individual as we are. Who can say what normal is? So if we are trying to live a "normal" life, it's probably based on a lie that Satan has told us. When we believe him and live in this world, we will surely die.

So remember that normal is just a setting on a washing machine. When we try to be normal, we miss out on God's gifts, and we will surely die. So embrace being one of a kind and live the life that God has planned just for you.

Happiness

*"A happy person is not a person in a certain
set of circumstances, but rather a person with
a certain set of attitudes." – Hugh Downs*

Happiness is that feeling that comes over you when you know life is good and you can't help but smile.

Happiness is a sense of well-being, joy, or contentment. When people are successful or safe or lucky, they feel happiness. The "pursuit of happiness" is something this country is based on, and different people feel happiness for different reasons. Whenever doing something causes happiness, people usually want to do more of it. No one ever complains about too much happiness.

I've had the quotes, definition, and scripture to this devotion in place for a number of days, but I have avoided writing about it until now. I guess that's because it deals with a subject that I struggle with. So in a way, I'm writing this for myself.

Happiness. We know what it is. We might even know when we are happy, but staying happy is a different story. Now we all have moments of happiness. It might be when we're fishing or pursuing another hobby. My happy activities are hunting, farming, and rodeo, but what I really want to focus on is complete happiness in life. Is that even possible? I think it's possible, but rare. The thing is that most of us don't know how to go about it. I mean we know that we are supposed to trust in God because of what He tells us in **Jeremiah 29:11**, but it's not that easy to do. To be honest, I've had times that I hated my life. I've wondered if God had forgotten about me, or if He just intended for me to be miserable for the rest of my life. I was having one of those days last week, and as I prayed about it, God directed me to this scripture.

Ecclesiastes 2:1-26. "I said to myself, 'I should have fun—I should enjoy everything as much as I can.' But I learned that this is also useless. It is foolish to laugh all the time. Having fun does not do any good. So I decided to fill my body with wine while I filled my mind with wisdom. I tried this foolishness because I wanted to find a way to be happy. I wanted to see what was good for people to do during their few days of life. Then I began doing great things. I built houses, and I planted vineyards for myself. I planted gardens, and I made parks. I planted all kinds of fruit trees. I made pools of water for myself, and I used them to water my growing trees. I bought men and women slaves, and there were slaves born in my house. I owned many great

things. I had herds of cattle and flocks of sheep. I
owned more things than any other person in
Jerusalem did. I also gathered silver and gold for
myself. I took treasures from kings and their nations.
I had men and women singing for me. I had
everything any man could want. I became very rich
and famous. I was greater than anyone who lived in
Jerusalem before me. My wisdom was always there to
help me. Anything my eyes saw and wanted, I got for
myself. My mind was pleased with everything I did.
And this happiness was the reward for all my hard
work. But then I looked at everything I had done and
the wealth I had gained. I decided it was all a waste of
time! It was like trying to catch the wind. There is
nothing to gain from anything we do in this life. Then
I decided to think about what it means to be wise or
to be foolish or to do crazy things. And I thought
about the one who will be the next king. The new
king will do the same as the kings before him. I saw
that wisdom is better than foolishness in the same
way that light is better than darkness. Wise people use
their minds like eyes to see where they are going. But
for fools, it is as if they are walking in the dark. I also
saw that fools and wise people both end the same
way. I thought to myself, 'The same thing that
happens to a fool will also happen to me. So why
have I tried so hard to become wise?' I said to myself,

'Being wise is also useless.' Whether people are wise or foolish, they will still die, and no one will remember either one of them forever. In the future, people will forget everything both of them did. So the two are really the same. This made me hate life. It was depressing to think that everything in this life is useless, like trying to catch the wind. I began to hate all the hard work I had done, because I saw that the people who live after me would get the things that I worked for. I will not be able to take them with me. Some other person will control everything I worked and studied for. And I don't know if that person will be wise or foolish. This is also senseless. So I became sad about all the work I had done. People can work hard using all their wisdom and knowledge and skill. But they will die and other people will get the things they worked for. They did not do the work, but they will get everything. That makes me very sad. It is also not fair and is senseless. What do people really have after all their work and struggling in this life? Throughout their life, they have pain, frustrations, and hard work. Even at night, a person's mind does not rest. This is also senseless. There is no one who has tried to enjoy life more than I have. And this is what I learned: The best thing people can do is eat, drink, and enjoy the work they must do. I also saw that this comes from God. If people do good and please God, He will give them wisdom, knowledge, and joy. But those who sin will get only the work of gathering and carrying things. God takes from the bad person and gives to the good person. But all this work is useless. It is like trying to catch the wind."

After reading this I figured out why I wasn't happy. It was all my fault. I listened to the enemy when he told me that I needed more or deserved more. I got to doing things for my gain, to say look what I did. I think we all fall into this. Because we are flesh, we are selfish, and we can be tricked easily into thinking in the "me first" way. The thing I figured out was a lot like King Solomon did. I could have the best farm, win the most awards, or make barrels of money, but just as Solomon said, all of that is material, and I would only be left wanting more.

So where is true happiness? I know and have known that it is in Jesus, but now I feel like I have more of a plan. When we finally realize that no matter how hard we work and fight we cannot beat the world alone, we really start to live. It's really easy to trust God with our salvation and eternal life, but it is hard to trust Him with our day-to-day stuff. This walk isn't easy, and we will stumble, but just remember Who is the keeper of happiness.

Relationship Advice

A young man asked his father how to find the right girl in life. His father told him not to worry about finding the right girl, but that he should focus on God's Will, and He would lead him to the right woman.

Relationships are certainly an experience. Some are great, some are good, and others are just plain terrible. At times you might experience all of these within a very short time. When it comes to dating, things can get really confusing. While I sure have made a bunch of mistakes in relationships, I have learned a few things, too. I want to pass this along. Most of the writing that I have found is geared toward the girls and how they should approach relationships. I hope that this might help some of the young men.

Okay boys, the top thing that we have to understand is that we are to grow up to be men. This might be confusing, so let's look at what it means. Being a man isn't necessarily an age thing. I know a couple of males who are "manhood age" but act like boys. To be a man, we have to understand a few things:

1. We have to understand that the world doesn't revolve around us.

2. We have to be willing to take responsibility for ourselves and be willing to provide for those who depend on us.
3. We have to have integrity—doing what is right even when no one is looking.
4. The most important thing is that we SEEK GOD'S WILL.

One of the most beautiful things that God created was a woman. This can lead a guy to a bunch of trouble. When we are young, it's hard to know how to handle some of the feelings that might come when we are starting a relationship. Boys, I want to share this with you.

2 Timothy 2:21-22. "If you keep yourself pure, you will be a special utensil for honorable use. Your life will be clean, and you will be ready for the Master to use you for every good work. Run from anything that stimulates youthful lusts. Instead, pursue righteous living, faithfulness, love, and peace. Enjoy the companionship of those who call on the Lord with pure hearts."

If you think that sex is how you get someone to like you, please talk to a trusted pastor or someone else you trust. Yes, God created sex; but He created it for couples who are married. Boys, it's not real manly to sleep with a lot of women. Look at it this way: God created sex as the great gift that a married couple gives to each other. When we don't respect that, we devalue that gift.

1 Corinthians 5:11. "I meant that you are not to associate with anyone who claims to be a believer yet indulges in sexual sin, or is greedy, or worships idols, or is abusive, or is a drunkard, or cheats people. Don't even eat with such people."

Paul tells us not to have anything to do with people who do these things. Guys, one thing that follows you is your reputation. How do you want to be known? Are you the kind that a father would want driving his daughter around? You might not be worried about this, but this is an important part of being a man, because it shows that you have respect for others, and more importantly, respect for yourself.

1 Corinthians 6:13-20. "You say, 'Food was made for the stomach, and the stomach for food.' This is true, though someday God will do away with both of them. But you can't say that our bodies were made for sexual immorality. They were made for the Lord, and the Lord cares about our bodies. And God will raise us from the dead by his power, just as he raised our Lord from the dead. Don't you realize that your bodies are actually parts of Christ? Should a man take his body, which is part of Christ, and join it to a prostitute? Never! And don't you realize that if a man joins himself to a prostitute, he becomes one body with her? For the Scriptures say, 'The two are united into one.' But the person who is joined to the Lord is one spirit with him. Run from sexual sin! No other sin so clearly affects the body as this one does. For sexual immorality is a sin against your own body. Don't you realize that your body is the temple of the Holy Spirit, who lives in you and was given to you by God? You do not belong to yourself, for God bought you with a high price. So you must honor God with your body."

It's important that we remember the last part of this verse. God created us, then Jesus died for us so we owe obedience to Him. One of the weirdest things that I have heard about from young people is texting inappropriate pictures. I'm not sure how this got so big, but guys look at the value of your body. A Man died for you. Don't disrespect Him and yourself by selling yourself so cheap. If the girl you are talking to is ok with this, you need to think about if y'all have the same values.

Men be proud of who you are, and remember to always seek God. He had the best in mind for those who believe in Him. Don't cheapen this by giving in to the world.

Talk Is Cheap

Matthew 9:4-5, 7. "Jesus knew what they were thinking and asked them, 'Why are you thinking such evil thoughts? I, the Messiah, have the authority on earth to forgive sins. But talk is cheap—anybody could say that. So I'll prove it to you by healing this man.' Then, turning to the paralyzed man, he commanded, 'Pick up your stretcher and go on home, for you are healed.' And the man jumped up and left!"

Talk is cheap. Jesus just didn't talk about it, He <u>was</u> about it. Today, let's be like Jesus and not just talk about Him, but let's Be About Him!!!!!

Peace Keepers

*"A generation which ignores history has no
past and no future." – Robert Heinlein*

This afternoon we went on a tour of
Oklahoma City. We went to the Oklahoma City
Federal Memorial and the Oklahoma City Stockyards.
That might not seem very important but as I looked
at the sights that we went to, I realized something. All
of this evil and terrorism in this world is bad, but it's
nothing new. On April 19, 1995, the Alfred P. Murrah
Federal Building was bombed by some low-down
folks who had a U-Haul truck and some common
farming supplies. There were 168 people confirmed
dead and almost 700 wounded. It seems like we
almost forgot that. It happened 21 years ago. Let me
tell you, there are people who come pray at the wall
there. They still bring cards and gifts, but how many
other people even think about it?

From the memorial we went to the
stockyards, established in 1918. There is no telling
how many fortunes were made and lost there. What
did we find when we drove out there? Cattle getting
worked, loaded, and moved. They were still doing
what they do.

All through this trip, I noticed law enforcement. Those folks are still out doing their best to do their jobs. Peacekeepers have always had a place and they always will.

Ecclesiastes 1:9-11. "All things continue the way they have been since the beginning. The same things will be done that have always been done. There is nothing new in this life. Someone might say, 'Look, this is new,' but that thing has always been here. It was here before we were. People don't remember what happened long ago. In the future, they will not remember what is happening now. And later, other people will not remember what the people before them did."

You might be thinking the murder rate is terrible. How could it have been worse? Murder has been around since the second generation of people on earth.

Genesis 4:8. "Cain said to his brother Abel, 'Let's go out to the field.' So they went to the field. Then Cain attacked his brother Abel and killed him.'"

So where does this hate come from? They didn't have guns back then, but there was murder. So what causes it?

Mark 7:20-23. "And Jesus said, 'The things that make people wrong are the things that come from the inside. All these bad things begin inside a person, in the mind: bad thoughts, sexual sins, stealing, murder, adultery, greed, doing bad things to people, lying, doing things that are morally wrong, jealousy, insulting people, proud talking, and foolish living. These evil things come from inside a person. And these are the things that make people unacceptable to God.'"

It comes from inside of us. It's not about weapons or technology. The feelings and desires that lead people to do both harm and help come from within each of us.

You might not think that they had to deal with terrorism back then; that it has to be something new. Not so; if you read in the Bible, you can find many incidents of attacks because people were different. Even the Apostle Paul was thought to be a terrorist at one time. In fact, before he turned his life over to God, he was a terrorist.

Acts 21:37-38. "When the soldiers were ready to take Paul into the army building, he asked the commander, 'Can I say something to you?' The commander said, 'Oh, you speak Greek? Then you are not the man I thought you were. I thought you were the Egyptian who started some trouble against the government not long ago and led four thousand terrorists out to the desert.'"

The thing that gives me hope is that even during those trying times in the Bible there were people who were still working with God's creatures just like I saw them do today.

Genesis 4:2. "Eve gave birth again to Cain's brother Abel. Abel became a shepherd, and Cain became a farmer."

Psalm 8:6-7. "You put them in charge of everything you made. You put everything under their control. People rule over the sheep and cattle and all the wild animals."

I felt a renewed faith that as long as God has believers here on earth, there will be people taking care of His animals. However, a certain sadness touched me as well when I thought about how violence and hate has been present since Cain and Abel, and even doubt and selfishness was present in the garden.

Matthew 5:9-10. "Great blessings belong to those who work to bring peace. God will call them his sons and daughters. Great blessings belong to those who suffer persecution for doing what is right. God's kingdom belongs to them."

I hope that our lives will someday see a time when we won't need a peacekeeper, when the hate and jealousy are overcome by folks just living for God and not trying to outdo others; but until then, I am thankful for those who risk their lives to protect us. I know that there are bad folks who are in that line of work, but now I hope you can see that the evil they show doesn't come from a job or an object but through the evil inside of us all. Instead of persecuting them, we should lift them up and help them find peace and accountability in their lives.

Nothing in this world is new, but I think that it can be new in us. We just need to understand that it's our choice to change and to seek His will.

In His Image

*"Whoever in prayer can say, 'Our Father,'
acknowledges and should feel the brotherhood
of the whole race of mankind."
— Tryon Edwards*

I'm troubled. Growing up in a small town we had friends. We didn't really have white friends and black friends. We just had friends. In my life now, I work with people from many different ethnic backgrounds. I can say that this is one of my favorite parts of my job. It does surprise me though when people in 2016 want to say that one race is superior or inferior to another. I hurts me to see this. When it comes from a person who doesn't know Christ, I am hurt; but when a person who claims a relationship with Jesus acts this way, I get angry. It makes me mad! All a person has to do is look in God's Word to find that God created each of us in His own image.

Genesis 1:26-28. "Then God said, 'Now let's make humans who will be like us. They will rule over all the fish in the sea and the birds in the air. They will rule over all the large animals and all the little things that crawl on the earth.' So God created humans in his own image. He created them to be like himself. He created them male and female. God blessed them and said to them, 'Have many children. Fill the earth and take control of it. Rule over the fish in the sea and the birds in the air. Rule over every living thing that moves on the earth.'"

Nowhere in that scripture nor in my Bible have I found where one skin color is superior to another. I've heard some say that certain ethnic groups might not get to Heaven. This isn't true at all. Let's look at what John says in Revelation.

Revelation 5:9-10. "And they all sang a new song to the Lamb: 'You are worthy to take the scroll and to open its seals, because you were killed, and with your blood sacrifice you bought people for God from every tribe, language, race of people, and nation. You made them to be a kingdom and to be priests for our God. And they will rule on the earth.'"

Revelation 7:9-10. "Then I looked, and there was a large crowd of people. There were so many people that no one could count them all. They were from every nation, tribe, race of people, and language of the earth. They were standing before the throne and before the Lamb. They all wore white robes and had palm branches in their hands. They shouted loudly, 'Victory belongs to our God, who sits on the throne, and to the Lamb.'"

Revelation 14:6. "Then I saw another angel flying high in the air. The angel had the eternal Good

News to announce to the people living on earth—to every nation, tribe, language, and race of people."

At least three times, John talks about Heaven and who you will see from every nation, tribe, and race of people. I believe that if you don't like jumping and shouting worship, then you are going to be in for a surprise.

Things that happened in the past can't be undone. Things that were done in generations past weren't good at times, and no amount of apology or repayment can make it better now. To be honest, most of us today had nothing to do with what happened in the past. The way that I believe we overcome this is not let it continue to happen or not let it happen again. We must see each other the way God sees us, no one better than another because of their skin color and background.

Amos 4:13. "He is the one who made the mountains. He created the wind. He lets people know his thoughts. He changes the darkness into dawn. He walks over the mountains of the earth. His name is Yahweh, Lord God All-Powerful."

The way we overcome the dark past and improve on today is to get back to seeking God and the plan that He has for us. We also must not tolerate mistreatment from anyone towards anyone regardless of ethnicity and appearance.

The Fourth of July

"I prefer peace. But if trouble must come, let it come in my time, so that my children can live in peace." — Thomas Payne

Some 240 years ago, a group of men and women put into action a leap of faith. They put into motion an awesome idea of freedom. During those 240 years, America has grown from 13 colonies to 50 states. However, the pride of country and the desire for freedom is still strong. The one thing that has remained constant is that freedom is by no means free. From Alaska to Florida and Maine to Hawaii, men and women from every city and fork in the road have been giving their liberty, freedom, and all too often, their lives to ensure that the sacrifices of those before them were not in vain and that America would continue to be free.

John 15:12-13. "This is what I command you: Love each other as I have loved you. The greatest love people can show is to die for their friends."

In the world today, some in this country take our freedom for granted. They seem not to understand that every decision and freedom we have here was paid for by someone's husband, wife, mother, father, brother, sister, son, or daughter. Some came home needing surgery, while some came home with wounds no one can see, and then there are others who didn't come home at all.

So today as we celebrate, please remember these costs. I would just ask that for today let's put aside being a Democrat, a Republican, or an Independent and just focus on being an American.

"I pledge allegiance to the flag of the United States of America, and to the republic for which it stands, one nation under God, indivisible, with liberty and justice for all."

Are You in the Right Flock?

"Birds of a feather flock together."
— Unknown.

Growing up in the country and on a farm it was common to see animals in groups. They might be called herds or flocks, but they are a group of animals that look out for and support each other. I've had cows that alert the others in danger. I've had goats that would nurse four or more babies. If you've ever seen a flock of chickens catch a snake, then you know how they work together. Animals need each other to survive. God created these for a purpose. The most important thing these flocks provide to us is nourishment.

Deuteronomy 32:13-14. "The Lord helped them take control of the hill country. They took the harvest in the fields. He gave them honey from the cliffs and olive oil from the rocky ground. He gave his people butter from the herd and milk from the flock. He gave them lambs and goats. They had the best rams from Bashan and the finest wheat. They drank the best wine made from the juice of red grapes."

The Lord provided physical nourishment to His people through His herds and flocks. We still have that today. We know that God sent Jesus to die for our sins and give an offer of salvation. However, God is so much more and so all knowing that He knows that we are like sheep. In fact, that's what He calls us, His sheep. So He knows that we have that flock mentality that's why He instructs us to help and support each other not only physically but with our spiritual needs as well. He says that when we are together in a group that He's with us.

Matthew 18:19-20. "To say it another way, if two of you on earth agree on anything you pray for, my Father in heaven will do what you ask. Yes, if two or three people are together believing in me, I am there with them."

My question to you is this, is the group, the herd, the flock that we find ourselves in, does it support us? Does this flock feed you? Protect you? Does it allow you to do all of these things for others? If not, it may be time for a change. It's these groups that help learn and to grow. They also help pick us up when we're down. Just remember it's better to be in a flock of His sheep than in a flock of buzzards who only think about themselves.

The Fickle Finger of Fate

I was listening to *Radio Classics* on my radio the other day. Most of these programs were made from 1940-1955. Anyway, I like the old stuff. I got this title from a Jack Benny show. Normally I would not pay much attention to words like that, but there was something about them that stuck with me. The more I thought on it, the more I realized many people have their lives described in those four words. I bet if we were to take an honest assessment of our own lives, most of us would find that, at some time or another, we have all lived our lives under the fickle finger of fate.

So here's what I did. I used a search function on my Bible app to look for those words. Fickle Finger of Fate. Well would you believe that those words aren't exactly used in the scriptures. Not to be deterred, I used one of those prehistoric things called a thesaurus. So let's look at what this title breaks down like.

Fickle – this was one word that I couldn't find, so I looked up indecisive. The action that fuels fickle and indecisive is doubt. We might doubt lots of things, how something will turn out or we might doubt that we will find happiness. Let's look at what James says about doubt.

James 1:6-7. "But when you ask God, you must believe. Don't doubt him. Whoever doubts is like a wave in the sea that is blown up and down by the wind. People like that are thinking two different things at the same time. They can never decide what to do. So they should not think they will receive anything from the Lord."

We shouldn't expect anything from God if we can't make up our minds. So look at it this way . . . being fickle can cost us blessings from God.

Finger – we have them on our hands. We use them for touch and feel. Oftentimes we use them as another way to make sure that something is real. Sometimes this is a good idea. We want to know the temperature of our bathwater or maybe to make sure that a chair is solid, but when it comes to faith in Jesus, we can't be like that. We have to have faith or believe in something that we can't see or touch. Look at what Jesus told Thomas.

John 20:25-29. "They told him, 'We saw the Lord.' Thomas said, 'That's hard to believe. I will have to see the nail holes in his hands, put my finger where the nails were, and put my hand into his side. Only then will I believe it.' A week later the followers were in the house again, and Thomas was with them. The doors were locked, but Jesus came and stood among them. He said, 'Peace be with you!' Then he said to Thomas, 'Put your finger here. Look at my hands. Put your hand here in my side. Stop doubting and believe.' Thomas said to Jesus, 'My Lord and my God!' Jesus said to him, 'You believe because you see me. Great blessings belong to the people who believe without seeing me!'"

Great blessings belong to those who believe in Jesus without seeing Him. Again doubt snuck in and can hold us back from the great things that Jesus has for use.

Fate – What the future holds or at least what will be the foundation for the future. I had trouble with this word but one of the synonyms was portion. How much of something that we will receive. It could be food or fortune that we will be given or inheriting. Look at the conversation between Joseph and his father.

Genesis 48:21-22. "Then Israel said to Joseph, 'Look, my time to die is almost here, but God will still be with you. He will lead you back to the land of your ancestors. I have given you one portion more than I gave to your brothers. I gave you the land that I won from the Amorites. I used my sword and bow to take that land.'"

I'm sure that there was some wonder in Joseph about what he might receive. He was concerned about his fate.

What are we to do? What can give us strength to keep our faith? We need only look at the scriptures.

Luke 1:37. "God can do anything!"

This one verse should tell us all that we need to know. God made this world and everything in it. To do this it has to mean that He is above or more than this world so He can do whatever He wants whenever He wants.

Romans 8:29-32. "God knew them before he made the world. And he decided that they would be like his Son. Then Jesus would be the firstborn of many brothers and sisters. God planned for them to be like his Son. He chose them and made them right with him. And after he made them right, he gave them his glory. So what should we say about this? If God is for us, no one can stand against us. And God is with us. He even let his own Son suffer for us. God gave his Son for all of us. So now with Jesus, God will surely give us all things."

Jeremiah 29:11-13. "I say this because I know the plans that I have for you." This message is from the Lord. "I have good plans for you. I don't plan to hurt you. I plan to give you hope and a good future. Then you will call my name. You will come to me and pray to me, and I will listen to you. You will search for me, and when you search for me with all your heart, you will find me."

If God is for us who can be against us? Satan? No, because God created him. The only way that Satan's way wins is when we give up on God, because you can take it to the bank God won't give up on us.

If you still wonder how much God loves each of us look no further than this.

John 3:15-17. "Then everyone who believes in Him can have eternal life. Yes, God loved the world so much that he gave his only Son, so that everyone who believes in him would not be lost but have eternal life. God sent his Son into the world. He did not send him to judge the world guilty, but to save the world through him."

Would you sacrifice your child for anyone? How about people that disrespect you, hate you, and otherwise take advantage of you? No!! But God did. If He is going to do that, he won't give up on us.

Father, thank you for this day. Thank you for giving us life. Father, please forgive us when we doubt. Father, please give us strength and wisdom to overcome worry and doubt. Father, please place your hands in our ears and over our eyes to block out Satan's attempts to cause us to second guess Your love for us. Amen!

There Is Still Work to Do

"Unplowed fields make hollow bellies;
unread books make hollow minds." –
Unknown

I have used lots of sayings. When I use the following saying, someone usually looks at me like I've got a third eye. When anyone asks if I've been working a lot, my answer is, "I've been hooked up short." Most people have no idea what this saying means and even fewer know where it comes from. So here's a little lesson. When farmers would plow their fields with horses or other animals, they would hook up the animal to the plow. When you hook them up short, it means that the plow is really in the ground and it takes a lot of effort to pull it. The looser or longer the animal is hooked up, the easier they have it, and they don't have to pull so hard. The problem is that the rows aren't very deep or straight. It might also take more time to get the job done. How do you think God wants us to be? Does he want us to do his work just half-heartedly or to do it right, even if that means working a little harder?

Jeremiah 4:3-4. "This is what the Lord says to the people of Judah and to Jerusalem: 'Your fields have not been plowed. Plow those fields! Don't plant seeds among the thorns. Become the Lord's people. Change your hearts. Men of Judah and people of Jerusalem, if you don't change, then I will become very angry. My anger will spread fast like a fire, and it will burn you up. No one will be able to put out that fire because of the evil you have done.'"

God tells these people that they have work to do. He wants us to do His work, and He wants us to do it right. That means if you are going to live for God, then live it right. Be straight and true in everything that we do. How do we accomplish this? We have to be "hooked up short," but not to just any plow; we have to be hooked up short and close to Jesus.

I know that some people think that when they accept Jesus and live for Him that they will be on "easy street." They might even quote this verse:

Matthew 11:28-30. "Come to me, all you who are weary and burdened, and I will give you rest. Take my yoke upon you and learn from me, for I am gentle and humble in heart, and you will find rest for your souls. For my yoke is easy and my burden is light."

He says that His yoke is easy and His burden is light, but He doesn't say you don't have to plow. The thing is folks, there is a cost for everything in life except for salvation because God gives us that through Grace. However, He has a plan for you and me. He wants to use us to let His greatness shine strong and true. When we live for Him, He makes the ground soft and the plow sharp, but we still have to go straight; the way to do that is be close to God in everything we do. So the key to living for God is that we need to be hooked up short.

Grow with Living Water

I'm a farmer. Anyone who knows me knows that I love farming. It doesn't matter to me if its plants, animals, fish, fruit, and now even indoor or outdoor. I love farming. It's not about making money, but it's about raising and nurturing something from nothing. You see, without a farmer, a newborn calf doesn't have much of a chance of living. A seedling probably won't survive without a farmer to water it and keep the weeds away. This is the time of year when planting is going on, the grass is greening up, and baby livestock is being born. The sad part is that in a few months, the cycle will start again, and the babies will be sold, and the plants will die off. That's kind of like our lives. We start out young and green but before long our bodies die off. Even so, there is a way for us to live on.

1 Peter 1:23-25. "You have been born again. This new life did not come from something that dies. It came from something that cannot die. You were born again through God's life-giving message that lasts forever. The Scriptures say, 'Our lives are like the grass of spring, and any glory we enjoy is like the beauty of a wildflower. The grass dries up and dies, and the flower falls to the ground. But the word of

the Lord lasts forever.' And that word is the Good
News that was told to you."

The word of God gives us the instructions
that if we believe in our hearts and confess with our
mouths that Jesus is Lord we will have everlasting life.
Just like a farmer faces drought and disease, our lives
won't be easy—just like farming isn't easy—but when
the end of the growing cycle is done and the harvest
is complete, the farmer can be happy with the results.
We can rejoice, knowing that if we do what God
wants us to, we will harvest the eternal life that He
has promised, when He tells us, "Well done my good
and faithful servant."

Are You All In?

There's a saying in life of "I'm all in." To be successful in life, I believe that you have to be all in with all that you do. I have been truly successful in few things in life, but in those things I was successful because I was fully committed to using the talents that God gave me. When I was learning to announce rodeos, I practiced daily. I have recordings of PRCA rodeos from the 90's. I have muted the tv and announced them many times. I've also been a pretty good farmer; the way I succeeded was that I listened to others and studied daily. In both of these activities, I also prayed a lot. I prayed that God would show me how to use my talents and to let me use them in a way that was pleasing to Him. Being a Christian following Jesus and to have eternal life in Heaven is no different. You have to be fully committed. You have to work, and above all, you have to pray. There are also some things we have to understand, and I'll explain that after the scripture.

Mark 10:17-31. "Jesus started to leave, but a man ran to him and bowed down on his knees before him. The man asked, 'Good Teacher, what must I do to get the life that never ends?' Jesus answered, 'Why do you call me good? Only God is good. And you know his commands: 'You must not murder anyone, you must not commit adultery, you must not steal, you must not lie, you must not cheat, you must respect your father and mother ….' The man said, 'Teacher, I have obeyed all these commands since I was a boy.' Jesus looked at the man in a way that showed how much he cared for him. He said, 'There is still one thing you need to do. Go and sell everything you have. Give the money to those who are poor, and you will have riches in heaven. Then come and follow me.' The man was upset when Jesus told him to give away his money. He didn't want to do this, because he was very rich. So he went away sad. Then Jesus looked at his followers and said to them, 'It will be very hard for a rich person to enter God's kingdom!' The followers were amazed at what Jesus said. But he said again, 'My children, it is very hard to enter God's kingdom! It is easier for a camel to go through the eye of a needle than for a rich person to enter God's kingdom!' The followers were even more amazed and said to each other, 'Then who can be saved?' Jesus looked at them and said, 'That is something people cannot do, but God can. He can do anything.' Peter said to Jesus, 'We left everything to follow you!' Jesus said, 'I can promise that everyone who has left their home, brothers, sisters, mother, father, children, or farm for me and for the Good News about me will get a hundred times more than they left. Here in this world they will get more homes, brothers, sisters, mothers, children, and farms. And with these things they will have persecutions. But in the world that is coming they will also get the reward of eternal life. Many people who have the highest place now will have the lowest place in the future. And the people who have the lowest place now will have the highest place then.'"

This young, rich man in the story; had a lot going for him; he was in a position that had some influence. The problem was that he wasn't all in. He looked at Jesus as a teacher and not as The Savior. The reason Jesus told him to give all of his things away was because Jesus knew that the young man's view on eternal life would always be centered on being able to buy his way in unless he had nothing. What the young man didn't understand was that when you follow Jesus and stay in His will, you have enough here on earth, not because you earned it, but because God blessed you with it through His love and grace. These can't be earned, they can only be given.

When we aren't living for Christ, nothing we do will lead us to fulfillment in life, and it sure won't lead to everlasting life. What we have to be is fully committed or "All In" to living for Christ. When we do this we will find true happiness and fulfillment in life on earth and eternal life with Jesus.

Be a Champion for The Lord

I've been in and around rodeo since I was 14 years old. I've had some great teachers and traveling partners. The number one thing that I learned from these people is that it's not always going to be easy, and you will get disgusted; but a true hand, a winner never gives up, they keep going and keep trying. While I have had some great examples in the arena, we all have the best example of how to live our lives.

Hebrews 12:1-3. "We have all these great people around us as examples. Their lives tell us what faith means. So we, too, should run the race that is before us and never quit. We should remove from our lives anything that would slow us down and the sin that so often makes us fall. We must never stop looking to Jesus. He is the leader of our faith, and he is the one who makes our faith complete. He suffered death on a cross. But he accepted the shame of the cross as if it were nothing because of the joy he could see waiting for him. And now he is sitting at the right side of God's throne. Think about Jesus. He patiently endured the angry insults that sinful people were shouting at him. Think about him so that you won't get discouraged and stop trying."

To be a champion cowboy/cowgirl you have to be focused. We are focused on being the best and we make sure that everything we do is working towards our goal. It could be hauling water from home to keep your horse drinking while on the road or carrying a companion horse to keep our good horse calm, it might be the Perfect Bit, the handmade saddle or custom pad, whatever works to keep us on top. Does that mean we will win all the time or we won't go into a slump? Haha, no we will still experience that but if we know we have prepared our best it's easier to keep our mind right and overcome.

In our lives, we must stay focused on Jesus. He is more precious than any gold buckle. We can stay focused on Him by finding those good traveling partners. In rodeo it's very common for rookies to hook up with veterans. This teaches the rookie how to stay focused. We must do this in life. We need that mentor to help us stay focused on Christ. They can help us stay away from the things that would cause us to stray. Jesus suffered unimaginably for us. He knew the goal. He now sits at the right hand of the Father. He could have quit, sold out to Satan. We know that since the Devil went after God's Son he's going to come after us. He will distract us, he will disgust us, and make us want to give up. But just like in the arena, we know we've worked, and we've prepared, and we can overcome. We know that when we follow the Will of God and believe in Jesus that we can overcome, and the reward for doing so will be paradise.

God Must Be a Farmer

I'M JUST A FARMER, PLAIN AND SIMPLE
by Bobby Collier

I'm just a farmer, plain and simple.
Not of royal birth, but rather a worker of the
earth.
I know not of riches, but rather of patches on
my britches.

I'm just a farmer, plain and simple.
I know of drought and rain, of pleasure and
pain.
I know the good, the bad, the happy and the
sad.
I'm a man of emotions.
A man who loves this land and the beauty of its
sand.

I'm just a farmer, plain and simple.
I know the spring's fresh flow and autumn's
golden glow.
Of a new born calf's hesitation and an eagle's
destination.

I'm just a farmer, plain and simple.
I know of tall pines and long waiting lines.
I know the warmth of campfires and the agony
of flat tires.

I'm just a farmer, plain and simple.
I'm a man who loves his job.
And the life that I live.

I'm just a farmer, plain and simple.
And I'm a reaper of harvest.
I'm the sower of seeds and I'm the tender of
stock.

I'm just a farmer, plain and simple.
I know of planting corn and bailing hay and
animals going astray.
I live in a complex world, but my faith guides
me.

I'm just a farmer, plain and simple.
I am a man who works with God.
I cannot succeed without his help.
For you see, I'm just a farmer, plain and simple.

I will always be a farmer at heart. I can
remember growing up how we would all gather on
Christmas Day at my Grandparents' house for a late
lunch and opening gifts. Then we would start our
evening milking. I remember looking up at the stars
as I fed the last of my bottle baby calves and thinking
about the night the Angels came to those shepherds .
. . wondering if their night was similar to mine. Today,
farmers aren't thought of too highly in some circles,
but on this night some two thousand years ago,
farmers (shepherds) were the ones chosen to
welcome Jesus Christ to Earth.

Luke 2:1-21. "And it came to pass in those
days, that there went out a decree from Caesar

Augustus that all the world should be taxed. And this taxing was first made when Cyrenius was governor of Syria. And all went to be taxed, every one into his own city. And Joseph also went up from Galilee, out of the city of Nazareth, into Judaea, unto the city of David, which is called Bethlehem; because he was of the house and lineage of David: To be taxed with Mary his espoused wife, being great with child. And so it was, that, while they were there, the days were accomplished that she should be delivered. And she brought forth her firstborn son, and wrapped him in swaddling clothes, and laid him in a manger; because there was no room for them in the inn. And there were in the same country shepherds abiding in the field, keeping watch over their flock by night. And, lo, the angel of the Lord came upon them, and the glory of the Lord shone round about them: and they were sore afraid. And the angel said unto them, Fear not: for, behold, I bring you good tidings of great joy, which shall be to all people. For unto you is born this day in the city of David, a Saviour, which is Christ the Lord. And this shall be a sign unto you; Ye shall find the babe wrapped in swaddling clothes, lying in a manger. And suddenly there was with the angel a multitude of the heavenly host praising God, and saying, Glory to God in the highest, and on earth peace, good will toward men. And it came to pass, as the angels were gone away from them into heaven, the shepherds said one to another, Let us now go even unto Bethlehem, and see this thing which is come to pass, which the Lord hath made known unto us. And they came with haste, and found Mary, and Joseph, and the babe lying in a manger. And when they had seen it, they made known abroad the saying which was told them concerning this child. And all they that heard it wondered at those things which were told them by the shepherds. But Mary kept all these things, and pondered them in her heart. And the shepherds returned, glorifying and praising God for all the things that they had heard and seen, as it was told unto them. And when eight days were accomplished for the circumcising of the child, his name was called Jesus, which was so named of the angel before he was conceived in the womb."

A baby born of a virgin. The one who came that through Him the world might find salvation. Was He born in a palace? Was He born on fine bedding in a warm, dry house? No the King of Kings and Lord of Lords was born in a stable, a barn where common farm animals were kept. He was lain in a feed trough that just hours, maybe minutes before, a cow or horse or donkey was eating out of.

If this were today, folks would throw a fit or at least say they were a victim of something or other, but for Jesus this was all by design. Part of the world's greatest saving plan. Because, as you can see, farmers are plain and simple. We work and toil and know that even the smallest and weakest of all is just as important as the biggest and the strongest. Jesus was born this night so many years ago to offer salvation to the world. <u>All</u> of the world . . . the smallest, the weakest, the poorest, as well as the biggest, the strongest, and the richest. Please enjoy this time of year and remember that on this night a child was born who would have to die for us to live.

Keep Looking for the Good in Life

I often wonder what's coming. Even as discouraging as life gets, I get excited thinking about what God has in store. I look at our country, and yes, I see some folks making terrible choices, but I know that God has a plan.

Habakkuk 1:2-11. "How long, O Lord, must I call for help? But you do not listen! 'Violence is everywhere!' I cry, but you do not come to save. Must I forever see these evil deeds? Why must I watch all this misery? Wherever I look, I see destruction and violence. I am surrounded by people who love to argue and fight. The law has become paralyzed, and there is no justice in the courts. The wicked far outnumber the righteous, so that justice has become perverted. The Lord replied, 'Look around at the nations; look and be amazed! For I am doing something in your own day, something you wouldn't believe even if someone told you about it. I am raising up the Babylonians, a cruel and violent people. They will march across the world and conquer other lands. They are notorious for their cruelty and do whatever they like. Their horses are swifter than cheetahs and fiercer than wolves at dusk. Their charioteers charge from far away. Like eagles, they swoop down to devour their prey. On they come, all bent on violence.

Their hordes advance like a desert wind, sweeping captives ahead of them like sand. They scoff at kings and princes and scorn all their fortresses. They simply pile ramps of earth against their walls and capture them! They sweep past like the wind and are gone. But they are deeply guilty, for their own strength is their god.'"

We see a lot of the same things happening today. It can get discouraging. The hard thing to do is continue to try to find the good. One of the greatest things we can do is lean on God and His promises. Just as God explains in the scriptures above, He has something working. We might not be able to see it, but He can see it. God promised to return one day— that's the great thing to me! So as we are faced with a world that wants to turn away from Him, we should be pushing harder than ever to help those around us develop a relationship with Him now. If you don't know Him as your savior, look me up, I can introduce you.

Monsters Are Real

*". . . Monsters are real,
and ghosts are real too. They live inside us,
and sometimes, they win." – Stephen King*

I never have liked scary movies. I never could watch them. I don't even like the idea of monsters or ghosts or zombies. I have always believed they never existed the way television and the movies portray them. Characters like Freddy Krueger, Jason Voorhees, or even the kinds of characters like we saw on *Ghostbusters*; but don't be fooled, they are real. Their existence is influenced by the worst monster of all—Satan.

What do these monsters look like? They take many forms. They might look like a job that places more importance on being the biggest or the best instead of doing things the right way. They might look like a dollar bill. I like money, but that's a monster that can take hold like no other. We know alcohol is a monster and drugs certainly are as well, but there are the quiet monsters like envy, jealousy, and bitterness. Since the Internet became mainstream, we have seen the monster of pornography grow. What about ghosts in life? As Stephen King says, they live within us. What does he mean? How many things have happened in our lives that we can't let go of? How many things do we regret, yet haven't forgiven ourselves for? These monsters and ghosts are real, and they bring evil wherever they go. We know that it can get discouraging when we are surrounded by so much evil in the world. Look at what Matthew says:

Matthew 24:12-13. "There will be so much more evil in the world that the love of most believers will grow cold. But the one who remains faithful to the end will be saved."

So what do we do? Just pray that we don't get caught up by one of these monsters? YES!! But if we do become afflicted, are we done for? No. Matthew also tells us this.

Matthew 4:24. "The news about Jesus spread all over Syria, and people brought to him all those who were sick. They were suffering from different kinds of diseases and pain. Some had demons inside them, some suffered from seizures, and some were paralyzed. Jesus healed them all."

Jesus is the true Ghostbuster. He drives out demons and slays monsters. We simply have to come to Him. Lean on Him. Give Him all of our problems. That's what he wants, but we also have to give Him our love and faith, and He will give us peace.

With Jesus We Can Be Fireproof

"Fire is the test of gold;
adversity, of strong men."
– Martha Graham

We have all heard the saying about "baptism by fire," or maybe "going from the frying pan into the fire." Sometimes life just feels like we've been thrown into a fire. What do we do? How can we face these troubled times? Our only true way to face and overcome these challenges is to be strong in our faith in God. When we stick to our guns on topics, you can bet there may be some upset people. Think about the story of Shadrach, Meshach, and Abednego. King Nebuchadnezzar had built an idol of gold and told all of his people that when they heard the music playing they were to bow to and worship the golden statue. These three fellows, Shadrach, Meshach, and Abednego, refused to do this. They stuck to their guns that there was only one true God. The king truly had them thrown into a fire that was so hot that it killed the men who were to put them in the furnace. This didn't faze these three. God sent an angel into the furnace to protect them.

Why were they not burned? Because they kept the faith. Would this have happened if these three guys had doubts about God? Probably not. I'm sure they might have been nervous, but they had no doubt that God's will would be done. That's the toughest part, trusting in God's will. The thing is, God's will is the best that can be; so when we keep the faith, we will be like Shadrach, Meshach, and Abednego when they came out of the fire. There was no burned hair or clothing or even a smell of smoke. The thing that did come from that fire was a stronger faith in God. That's the way we will be every time we're put into the fire and come out on the other side.

Satan: That Silver-Tongued Devil

I read an article recently that said a majority of Christians don't believe that Satan actually exists but the same article said that 97% of evangelical Christians believe in angels. That seems strange to me. How can we read The Word and say we believe in one and not in the other? I don't know if it's just not completely understanding the Bible or that they don't want to face the fact that there is someone who wants to pull us away from God and that there are defined consequences for sin. Well folks I want to tell you that Satan is real, and he does want to steal us away from God. In this devotional, I will try to explain who Satan is, why he does what he does, and introduce my next devotional, which will be how to make sure we are continually building a strong relationship with Christ.

I hear folks say a lot that they believe in Christ but that they don't regularly work on their relationship with Him. This concerns me. Satan wasn't created in Hell. Look at the following passage.

Ezekiel 28:12-18. "Son of man, sing this sad song about the king of Tyre. Say to him, 'This is what the Lord God says: 'You were the perfect man—so full of wisdom and perfectly handsome. You were in Eden, the garden of God. You had every precious stone—rubies, topaz, and diamonds, beryls, onyx, and jasper, sapphires, turquoise, and emeralds. And each of these stones was set in gold. You were given this beauty on the day you were created. God made you strong. You were one of the chosen Cherubs who spread your wings over my throne. I put you on the holy mountain of God. You walked among the jewels that sparkled like fire. You were good and honest when I created you, but then you became evil. Your business brought you many riches. But they also put cruelty inside you, and you sinned. So I treated you like something unclean and threw you off the mountain of God. You were one of the chosen Cherubs who spread your wings over my throne. But I forced you to leave the jewels that sparkled like fire. Your beauty made you proud. Your glory ruined your wisdom. So I threw you down to the ground, and now other kings stare at you. You did many wrong things. You were a very crooked merchant. In this way you made the holy places unclean. So I brought fire from inside you. It burned you! You burned to ashes on the ground. Now everyone can see your shame.'"

You can bet that Satan knows God. He believes in God. The passage says that Satan was an angel who sat over the throne. That is pretty close, but Satan wanted to be more than just an angel, and that's what got him kicked out of Heaven.

When this happened, Satan grew a very bad hatred for Christ, but he knew he couldn't fight God and win. He had already tried and lost. So he figures that he will beat God by playing on the free will that God gave us.

Matthew 4:1-11. "Then the Spirit led Jesus into the desert. He was taken there to be tempted by the devil. Jesus ate nothing for 40 days and nights. After this, he was very hungry. The devil came to tempt him and said, 'If you are the Son of God, tell these rocks to become bread.' Jesus answered him, 'The Scriptures say, "It is not just bread that keeps people alive. Their lives depend on what God says."' Then the devil led Jesus to the holy city of Jerusalem and put him on a high place at the edge of the Temple area. He said to Jesus, 'If you are the Son of God, jump off, because the Scriptures say, "God will command his angels to help you, and their hands will catch you, so that you will not hit your foot on a rock."' Jesus answered, 'The Scriptures also say, "You must not test the Lord your God."' Then the devil led Jesus to the top of a very high mountain and showed him all the kingdoms of the world and all the wonderful things in them. The devil said, 'If you will bow down and worship me, I will give you all these things.' Jesus said to him, 'Get away from me, Satan!' The Scriptures say, "You must worship the Lord your God. Serve only him!" So the devil left him. Then some angels came to Jesus and helped him."

He tempted Jesus!! That is brave. If he thinks that he could tempt God's own Son into following him, he feels that you and I are his for sure. If he succeeds, we will spend eternity with him. The Bible goes on to tell us that Satan will be thrown into The Lake of Fire, and he will burn forever and ever. Does that sound fun to you? There is a way to fight him off. Paul tells us in the following verses about the armor of the Lord.

Ephesians 6:13-18. "That is why you need to get God's full armor. Then on the day of evil, you will be able to stand strong. And when you have finished the whole fight, you will still be standing. So stand strong with the belt of truth tied around your waist, and on your chest wear the protection of right living. On your feet wear the Good News of peace to help you stand strong. And also use the shield of faith with which you can stop all the burning arrows that come from the Evil One. Accept God's salvation as your helmet. And take the sword of the Spirit—that sword is the teaching of God. Pray in the Spirit at all times. Pray with all kinds of prayers, and ask for everything you need. To do this you must always be ready. Never give up. Always pray for all of God's people."

Paul talks about God's salvation. Salvation is what is given to us by God's grace. Satan will try very hard to get us not to take the gift of salvation. That's why it is so important to keep God's armor around us.

Now that I have told you about Satan and that he is real, alive, and well, my next devotional will be on how we can build a relationship with Christ, put Satan in his place, and not let him rob us of the Grace of God.

The Blame Game

I've noticed as I've gotten older that when something happens, we are quick to point fingers. I'm as guilty as anyone. Do you think this is a new thing or a growing trend? I'm sorry to say that it's not. It's been around since Adam and Eve.

Genesis 3:6-13. "The woman could see that the tree was beautiful and the fruit looked so good to eat. She also liked the idea that it would make her wise. So she took some of the fruit from the tree and ate it. Her husband was there with her, so she gave him some of the fruit, and he ate it. Then it was as if their eyes opened, and they saw things differently. They saw that they were naked. So they got some fig leaves, sewed them together, and wore them for clothes. During the cool part of the day, the Lord God was walking in the garden. The man and the woman heard him, and they hid among the trees in the garden. The Lord God called to the man and said, 'Where are you?' The man said, 'I heard you walking in the garden, and I was afraid. I was naked, so I hid.' God said to the man, 'Who told you that you were naked? Did you eat fruit from that special tree? I told you not to eat from that tree!' The man said, 'The woman you put here with me gave me fruit from that tree. So I ate it.' Then the Lord God said to the woman, 'What have you done?' She said, 'The snake tricked me, so I ate the fruit.'"

See when God quizzed Adam, he blamed Eve, and then in turn, she blamed the snake. Was it really Eve's fault that Adam disobeyed? Was it really the snake's fault that Eve disobeyed? The answer is no. Then why would they do this? Why would they lie to God when they know He knows everything? That's what sin does. It fools us into thinking we can make ourselves look better if we can make someone else look bad.

Since Adam and Eve got kicked out of the garden and sin has prevailed, Satan has taken his place as the ruler of Earth.

2 Corinthians 4:4. "Satan, who is the god of this world, has blinded the minds of those who don't believe. They are unable to see the glorious light of the Good News. They don't understand this message about the glory of Christ, who is the exact likeness of God."

You see we have become blind to God's love and the beauty that only He can give us, so now we blame others. We can't get a good job, we blame the government. We don't have money, we blame the economy. We get hooked on drugs, we blame our culture. When in reality, we need only to look at ourselves. Did we work as hard as we could to get a job, not just a paycheck? Did we live within what we could afford, or live like we think we deserve? ("Deserve" will be the topic for another day.) Did we know what could happen if we took these pills or powder? Did you ask God for His direction? Did you submit to His will?

Sometimes we are blessed to be surrounded by friends that God has placed in our lives who will help us when we start getting blinded by Satan. Not only do they support us, but also hold us accountable for our actions. There are some who might say that's judgmental, but it's scriptural.

Galatians 6:1-5. "Brothers and sisters, someone in your group might do something wrong. You who are following the Spirit should go to the one who is sinning. Help make that person right again, and do it in a gentle way. But be careful, because you might be tempted to sin, too. Help each other with your troubles. When you do this, you are obeying the law of Christ. If you think you are too important to do this, you are only fooling yourself. Don't compare yourself with others. Just look at your own work to see if you have done anything to be proud of. You must each accept the responsibilities that are yours."

Paul tells these folks to help those who are sinning. I had this done to me the other day, and I was thankful for this man and his love for me. He helped me see where I had strayed. After we talked, I had a couple of choices. I could have ignored him, I could have found someone or something to blame it on, or I could have done what Paul tells these folks to do:

Galatians 6:5. "You must each accept the responsibilities that are yours."

I accepted it, took responsibility for my actions, and told Satan that I wasn't going to play his blame game.

Friends with Benefits

What can Ole Tom be talking about. He's bringing up some stuff that a God-fearing man shouldn't talk about. Well just hang on. Nowadays the title I used brings on thoughts that go to the gutter pretty quickly, but I want to tell you that if you have the right friends, the benefit can truly be Heaven eternal.

There is a benefit to having friends. They are someone to have lunch with or talk to or pull you out of a bind. I had an old car one time and on my way home from work, there is this awful racket. I pulled into a convenience store, not sure what was going on. Just as I was trying to figure some stuff out, here comes my friend Doug. He helps me figure it out, and I was on my way to get the wheel bearings changed. Doug helped me not because he had to but because he is my friend. I bet you can think of those people in your life who help you or who you help because they are your friend. Some of those friends even become like family.

Proverbs 17:17. "A friend loves at all times, and a brother is born for adversity."

Friends also keep us on the right track. I was attending a church close to my hometown. Well rodeo season came around, and I was out of town for several weekends in a row. After missing about four weeks, I got a call from one of my friends in the men's group there. He was calling to check on me, offer help and encouragement. Sometimes we even have friends who call us out when we have started following the world and not seeking Christ. It might cause some sparks, but if it's done right, we will be better for it.

Proverbs 27:17. "As iron sharpens iron, so a man sharpens the countenance of his friend."

If we surround ourselves with true friends who are like family, that helps us to keep seeking Christ, and we can see some great benefits.

Psalm 68:19-20. "Blessed be the Lord, Who daily loads us with benefits, The God of our salvation! Selah Our God is the God of salvation; And to GOD the Lord belong escapes from death."

King David knew that having those strong friends and being a friend with God would be the only way to escape death and have everlasting life.

Psalm 103:2-5. "Bless the Lord, O my soul, and forget not all His benefits: Who forgives all your iniquities, Who heals all your diseases, Who redeems your life from destruction, Who crowns you with lovingkindness and tender mercies, Who satisfies your mouth with good things, So that your youth is renewed like the eagle's."

To go along with the awesome saving grace, God also wants to give His friends great things in our lives while we are here on earth.

James 1:16-18. "Do not be deceived, my beloved brethren. Every good gift and every perfect gift is from above, and comes down from the Father of lights, with whom there is no variation or shadow of turning. Of His own will He brought us forth by the word of truth, that we might be a kind of first fruits of His creatures."

With the promise of eternal life through God's grace and the gifts and blessings that He wants to give us during our life, it should be everyone's goal to surround ourselves with like-minded people and do our best to be friends with God. That way we can help others in their walk with The Lord. That way we can have and be friends with benefits.

I Love Palm Trees

Today is Palm Sunday, the Sunday before Easter. Anymore, if you were to mention a palm tree, most people would think of the beach. Especially this time of year being spring break. We often think of beaches and Palm trees as the arrival of spring and summer. This is nice, but did you know that Palm branches were once used to welcome someone much more warm and bright than spring time?

John 12:12-13. "The next day a great multitude that had come to the feast, when they heard that Jesus was coming to Jerusalem, took branches of palm trees and went out to meet Him, and cried out: 'Hosanna! Blessed is He who comes in the name of the Lord! The King of Israel!'"

John 12:14-15. "Then Jesus, when He had found a young donkey, sat on it; as it is written: 'Fear not, daughter of Zion; Behold, your King is coming, Sitting on a donkey's colt.'"

To understand why this is significant, let's first look at what they did when they heard Jesus was coming up the road to Jerusalem. They were gathering for the Passover feast when the folks heard He was on His way. Back then it was customary to cover the road for someone of importance. The Greeks would rip up togas or whatever, but the Palm branch was used to symbolize victory. Some of those at that time used it to show victory over death and eternal life. But why in the world would He ride a donkey? I mean a big-eared, short-tailed, ugly donkey. Jesus sure could have found a nice horse to ride. I think the reasons that He chose a donkey are these: A donkey in that time was a symbol of peace. Even today as I watched an old Western movie, I saw a nun riding a donkey. Horses have a great power about them. A donkey is beast of burden, a pretty common animal that most everyone had. Jesus is the Prince of Peace, and He came to give His life so that each and every one of us could be saved.

John Wayne said that courage was being scared to death but saddling up anyway. I don't know if Jesus was scared as He rode that donkey into town, but I know each of us would have been. The folks got it right though. There was the most important Man who ever lived coming down that road. They used those Palm leaves to cover the road to honor Him. Just a few days later, He would use His blood to cover our sins. That's sure not a fair trade!

Folks I hope you know Him! Because before long, we are going to be covering the road again, and I sure love the look of those Palm leaves.

Follow the Coach's Plan

On my way home from work every day, I listen to a sports talk show. It never fails at least one time during my drive, I hear a caller ask, "Do y'all think we are going to have a quarterback that's better than the one we had last year? We've got four on the team. Any of them have got to be better than the one last year. I'll hang up and listen." The answer boils down to the same thing. The coach and his staff see the players each and every day, so we have to believe that they put the best out there. A lot of people agree; some don't, but a whole bunch do. In our own lives, we do this; we don't question the coach, though we question God.

I catch myself saying, "I wonder if God really knows what I'm going through or what's about to happen?" How stupid am I? This is the same God who spoke the world into being. (Genesis). The same one who made the sun stand still at the request of a human (Joshua) and the very same God who not only raised Lazarus from the dead, but died on the cross and came back three days later. That God is still on the job. He didn't retire, resign, get fired, or quit. He's still alive and all powerful. So why do we question Him? Just like in my last writing, we talked about Satan and how he talked Adam and Eve out of the

Garden. That's what he does to us. He talks. He lies. We listen. We doubt. We question God. That's how Satan works. If we wouldn't listen to him, he would have absolutely no power over us. So right now, I want to share just a few bits of information that shows that God is in control.

We have all seen this verse . . .

Philippians 4:13: "I can do all things through Christ who strengthens me."

We have probably all read this one . . .

Luke 1:37: "For with God nothing will be impossible."

That should be all we need right there. When you add in . . .

John 3:16: "For God so loved the world that He gave His only begotten Son, that whoever believes in Him should not perish but have everlasting life."

We should know that we are on the winning side, but some folks just use that as bulletin board material, so I have included these next three passages to prove that you never question the Coach. The coach will tell the players what they can expect.

Jeremiah 29:11. "I say this because I know the plans that I have for you." *(This message is from the Lord.)* "I have good plans for you. I don't plan to hurt you. I plan to give you hope and a good future."

A good coach takes responsibility when the players don't follow the game plan.

Isaiah 53:6. "We had all wandered away like sheep. We had gone our own way. And yet the Lord put all our guilt on Him."

And even when others can't see that diamond in the rough, a good coach keeps polishing away until even the most unlikely shine bright.

Acts 9:1-21. "In Jerusalem, Saul was still trying to scare the followers of the Lord, even saying he would kill them. He went to the high priest and asked him to write letters to the synagogues in the city of Damascus. Saul wanted the high priest to give him the authority to find people in Damascus who were followers of the Way. If he found any believers there, men or women, he would arrest them and bring them back to Jerusalem. So Saul went to Damascus. When he came near the city, a very bright light from heaven suddenly shined around him. He fell to the ground and heard a voice saying to him, 'Saul, Saul! Why are you persecuting me?' Saul said, 'Who are you, Lord?' The voice answered, 'I am Jesus, the one you are persecuting. Get up now and go into the city. Someone there will tell you what you must do.' The men traveling with Saul just stood there, unable to speak. They heard the voice, but they saw no one. Saul got up from the ground and opened his eyes, but he could not see. So the men with him held his hand and led him into Damascus. For three days, Saul could not see; he did not eat or drink. There was a follower of Jesus in Damascus named Ananias. In a vision the Lord said to him, 'Ananias!' Ananias answered, 'Here I am, Lord.' The Lord said to him, 'Get up and go to the street called Straight Street. Find the house of Judas and ask for a man named Saul from the city of Tarsus. He is there now, praying. He has seen a vision in which a man named Ananias came and laid his hands on him so that he could see again.' But Ananias answered, 'Lord, many people have told me about this man. They told me about the many bad things he did to your holy people in Jerusalem. Now he has come here to Damascus. The leading priests have given him the power to arrest all people who trust in you.' But the Lord Jesus said to Ananias, 'Go! I have chosen Saul for an important work. I want him to tell other nations, their rulers, and the people of Israel about me. I will show him all that he must suffer for me.' So Ananias left and went to the house of Judas. He laid his hands on Saul and said, 'Saul, my brother, the Lord Jesus sent me. He is the one you saw on the road when you came here. He sent me so that you can see again and also be filled with the Holy Spirit.' Immediately, something that looked like fish scales fell off Saul's eyes. He was able to see! Then he got up and was baptized. After he ate, he began to feel strong again. Saul stayed with the followers of Jesus in Damascus for a few days. Soon he began to go to the synagogues and tell people about Jesus. He told the people, 'Jesus is the Son of God!' All the people who heard Saul were amazed. They said, 'This is the same man who was in Jerusalem trying to destroy the people who trust in Jesus! And that's why he has come here—to arrest the followers of Jesus and take them back to the leading priests.'"

Saul became Paul and to see how he shined you just have to read the New Testament since he wrote most of it. The same God that did all of this is still calling the plays today. We don't need to doubt. He knows how to win. Put me in Coach, I'm ready!

Postscript

What you have read comes from a couple of years of conversations with God. I'm proud of these devotionals – not because I was able to write them, but because I have a God who loves me just the way I am and because He wants to have a relationship with me. He wants a relationship with you, too. I hope that you enjoyed these devotionals, and in some way, you found strength and a better relationship with God. We all have a responsibility to take care of His herd. I hope that, just as a dairy farmer would feed and care for his herd, this book helps to feed you. It does me.

Father, I thank You for the blessings that I have found in writing this book; I pray that You are honored by it. I ask that You give peace and understanding to all who read these words. Father, I pray that all who read each devotional find You. Amen.

Biography

Tom Harrington and his twin brother, Toby, were born in *(Month)* 19*??*, into a family of carpenters and dairy farmers. They grew up in the little town of Guy, Arkansas; a town so small that, at one time, the Harrington family had more cows than there were people who lived in Guy.

Although Tom was born with cerebral palsy, Toby always pushed him to do whatever he wanted to do, which led to some interesting situations. During high school, Tom and Toby became interested in rodeo. Tom was always one who could talk about anything, so he soon found himself announcing.

Tom always had a love for farming and has owned several cows, pigs, chickens, goats, and horses. He and Toby exhibited chickens at several fairs during high school. The success they had helped pay Tom's way through college.

When Tom graduated from high school and was about to go to college, some family members advised him that if he dropped out of college, the road didn't run home any longer. That was quite a motivator! In May of 2000, the same weekend he graduated from college, Tom's rodeo career took off as he announced his first big rodeo in Paris, Arkansas.

Tom's rodeo adventures have taken him all across the state of Arkansas, as well as to places in Missouri, Tennessee, Texas, and Oklahoma. He has won several awards for announcing and continues to travel to many rodeos each year.

Tom's love of agriculture led him to earn a Master's Degree from the University of Arkansas, and once again, he was back in Paris, Arkansas, announcing the rodeo on the very same weekend.

Tom has had many jobs, but the common theme was always that he was teaching others. This took Tom to the Arkansas Department of Correction, managing the dairy farm. Tom worked there for five years and met inmates from all different backgrounds. This is where *Ministry in the Milk barn* was born. On Sunday mornings while milking cows, Tom and some inmates would discuss the Word of God. Tom had experienced God throughout his life, but never as strongly as he did while he was milking cows at the prison.

In 2014, Tom married Leann Culp, and God moved him from the prison to the classroom where he spent three years mentoring troubled youth. Then in 2017, God moved Tom again; this time working with convicted felons to help them find jobs. Tom has also started preaching at some youth rodeos. Tom doesn't look at God as a religion but as a relationship. As Tom strives to build relationships with the people he meets, he wants to help others build a relationship with God.

Tom Harrington
Address
Phone Number
painehall@yahoo.com
Website: